T0209935

# Peace in the Midst of the Storm

*A Collection of Psalms and Poems*

## J. MICHAEL VESSELS

WestBow
PRESS®
A DIVISION OF THOMAS NELSON
& ZONDERVAN

Scripture taken from the New King James Version®. Copyright © 1982 by Thomas Nelson. Used by permission. All rights reserved.

This book is a work of non-fiction. Unless otherwise noted, the author and the publisher make no explicit guarantees as to the accuracy of the information contained in this book and in some cases, names of people and places have been altered to protect their privacy.

WestBow Press books may be ordered through booksellers or by contacting:

WestBow Press
A Division of Thomas Nelson & Zondervan
1663 Liberty Drive
Bloomington, IN 47403
www.westbowpress.com
1 (866) 928-1240

ISBN: 978-1-9736-3903-9 (sc)
ISBN: 978-1-9736-3904-6 (e)

Library of Congress Control Number: 2018910633

Print information available on the last page.

WestBow Press rev. date: 10/01/2018

A Gift Presented to

_____

From

_____

to
Dorris Vessels –
My mother
My friend
My teacher
My inspiration

A copy of this book is heaven-sent as she reads it at the feet of Jesus Christ her Lord, God, and Savior.

My friends if my loving, gentle, kind, mother, warrior for the king were here today she would tell you, she would say, she would declare, proclaim, "Praise my loving Lord, God, and Saviour! Jesus is the answer to all your sorrows! All your pain! All the inner turmoil that plagues you in the midnight hour!"

I have been deeply influenced by the inspiration of the Holy Spirit and my mother when she was alive to write this book to help you in your deepest sorrows of the heart in order to set you free.

Free at last!

Free at last!

Free at last!

By the blood of Jesus, the Lamb, and by the power of His righteous right hand.

# Contents

# Acknowledgment

A word of thanks to my friends who have encouraged me to copyright this work:

Hugh Herndon
My spiritual mentor, and advisor

Pastor Daniel G. Aleman
My source of encouragement

Pastor Dan Aleman and his wife Debbie
My Pastor, my friends, my teachers

Edie Thompson
My friend, my writing advisor

Dan Thompson
My friend, my business advisor

Marcy Vessels
My wife, my love, my best friend
Editor of this book

Jason Michael Vessels
My son, my friend, my joy
Technical advisor

Fear not, for I am with you; Be not dismayed, for I am your God. I will strengthen you, yes, I will help you, I will uphold you with My righteous right hand.

Isaiah 41:10

# Preface

Peace in the Midst of the Storm is a book for those who need comfort in a time of pain in their life. This is a series of poems, psalms, and teachings to help people to find their way in life and find the answers to the impossible problems of which only God Almighty Himself can solve.

I have made a special effort to bring peace, hope, love, kindness, and gentleness to people who are crying out to God. I want you to know my heart's desire is to tell you, the reader, that the answer is Jesus Christ, the Son of the Living God. You can always have more money, more material things, but nothing compares to the love of my loving Jesus. He bled for you, He cried for you, He gave all He had to give. He stepped out of heaven to step into your heart to rescue you from death, hell, and the grave. He is my king, the Great and the Mighty One, He is Lord, He is God, He is Savior. Shall I also speak to you of His mighty names? He is the Lion of Judah, the Rose of Sharon, the Bright and Morning Star, He is the King of Kings, Lord of Lords, He is the Everlasting One, the One who is worthy to be praised. He is the Lamb for the slaughter.

My dearest friends, I am the writer, you are the reader, and it is my honor to share with you my loving, gentle, kind, and compassionate Jesus Christ, the Son of the living God. He has helped me, delivered me, and rescued me so many times I cannot even count. I hope you will enjoy this book and remember that Jesus Christ, the Son of the Living God, is the answer to all of your problems. God bless you always.

# The Priestly Blessing

And the Lord spoke to Moses, saying: "Speak to Aaron and his sons, saying, 'This is the way you shall bless the children of Israel. Say to them:

"The Lord bless you and keep you;
The Lord make His face shine upon you,
And be gracious to you;
The Lord [e]lift up His countenance upon you,
And give you peace."

"So they shall [f]put My name on the children of Israel, and I will bless them."

Numbers 6:22-27

# Behold, the Glory of God!

Have you ever had problems in your life and did not know how, where, or when, to find the answers?

I'm a firm believer that there is a tailor-made answer for us in the Word of God. Yes, we do have to search for the answers diligently, but they are there like small nuggets of gold, promises of peace, hope, and love eternal. His Bible, His book, is like a map to success and victory in this life we live on earth.

When I am down and out and this old world starts crashing in on me with the pressures of living, I simply go outside and look up at the stars, the clouds, the moon, and the sky. I begin to admire and praise Him for the majesty of His beauty, His handiwork.

I start my journey with Jesus praising, worshipping, and magnifying His holy, precious name. I proclaim the wonderful promises of His Word compared to the vast universe He has created.

In order to solve your problems, you must trust, believe and know that He is bigger than any problem you could ever have. You see, my friend, you must focus on Jesus, the King of glory, the author and finisher of your life, the Creator of your very last breath.

**Scriptures:**

He is the image of the invisible God, the firstborn over all creation. For by Him all things were created that are in heaven and that are on earth, visible and invisible, whether thrones or dominions or principalities or powers. All things were created through Him and for Him. And He is before all things, and in Him all things consist.

Colossians 1:15-17

# Creation Cries Out

The sky declares Your glory.
The clouds, they shout to the heavens above.
The earth below, of Your majesty, Your power,
Your eternal being.
The sky, the clouds, join together in celebration
to praise,
honor,
magnify,
and worship Your holy, holy name.
They proclaim Your glory.
The rolling thunder cries out
that You are worthy to be praised.
The lightning dispels the darkness,
pushing it back, proclaiming,
I am that I am.
I am Lord God Almighty,
the great and the mighty one,
the holy, the just, and the fair one.
The majestic clouds shout out
with tears of joy,
love,
peace,
and tranquility,
dropping the rain from the heavens,
speaking in the tongue of creation,
You are Lord,
You are God.
Yes, You, and You alone are the God of
mercy,
grace,
love,
joy,
peace,

and the author of life,
all that is, and all that will be.
Yes Lord, You are King.
You are Savior.
You are holy.
You are the Creator.
You are the Redeemer.
You are the keeper of my heart,
my mind,
my body,
my soul,
and my spirit.
Yes, You are my God.
Forevermore,
Amen!

# Day by Day, Night by Night

Day by day, night by night,
the glory of the Lord is all about.
Day by day, night by night,
the angels in heaven above say,
"Holy, holy, holy, Lord God Almighty,
who was, and is, and is to come!"*
Day by day, night by night,
the twenty-four elders round about the throne of God say,
"You are worthy, o Lord,
to receive glory and honor and power,
for You created all things,
and by Your will they exist and you were created."**
Day by day, night by night,
the great and the mighty warriors of old
proclaimed,
"Praise the lord, for His mercy endures forever."***
This I say,
this I speak,
this I proclaim,
this I sing,
"As for me and my house, we will serve the Lord our God.
The Lion of Judah,
Emmanuel,
the great I Am,
the Rose of Sharon,
the bright and morning star."
Yes, I proclaim from the highest mountain,
upon every year,
upon every month,
upon every day,
upon every hour,
upon every minute,
upon every second,

upon every moment in time,
"Holy, holy, holy, Lord God almighty,
who was, and is, and is to come!"*
You are worthy, O Lord, to be praised,
to be gloried in,
to be honored,
and to be respected
for You are our King, our Savior,
by Your precious holy blood!
You are the eternal one, my God,
Jesus Christ, the Son of the living God.

* Revelation 4:8.
** Revelation 4:11.
*** Second Chronicles 20:21.

# High Upon this Mountain

High upon this mountain, all covered with snow,
the clouds of glory down below.
The seasons are changing from summer to fall,
green leaves falling as the winter it calls.

High upon this mountain, all covered in snow,
the clouds of glory down below.
The autumn winds they blow as
the fields,
the trees,
are on fire with
the presence,
the glory,
the grace of God's handiwork.

High upon this mountain, all covered with snow,
the clouds of glory down below.
Sunny bright mornings,
pale moon-lit nights keep me from feeling alone.

High upon this mountain of glory,
of peace,
of beauty,
I feel alive.
My heart,
my soul,
cry out a song of worship,
a song of praise,
a song of thanksgiving.
My mind it swells with the thoughts of
my Creator,
my Redeemer,
my Lord God and Savior,

the great and mighty King,
Jesus Christ the Son of the living God.
He is the lion of Judah,
the Rose of Sharon,
the great I Am.
He is the bright and morning star.
He is indeed the author of my life eternal
and all of this beauty that surrounds me.

High on this mountain all covered with snow,
the clouds of glory down below.
I gave up my final breath of life to heaven above.
It's time to go!

# Nature Cries Out

On the other side of midnight,
the darkness gives way to the light.
The trees, they clap their hands with praise.
The grass reaches up to meet the sky in thanksgiving.
The flowers touch the sunlight,
being fed by the worship of glory.
The sky surrenders to the wind as it proclaims that God is eternal,
the author and finisher of life itself.
The clouds of majesty, soft and pure,
they resound.
The rumbling, the sound of thunder
speaking the language of power and authority on the earth.
The lightning commands the sky above
and the valleys below,
to make way for the light to come forth.
The rocks, the ground, they rest in wait
for the presence of God almighty
to let the rain of heaven come down
upon their beings to have their ways.
The rivers, they flow, they rumble,
they proclaim "You are God!"
The oceans blue so deep, so pure, so magnificent,
they speak with
waves of thunder,
waves of glory,
waves of eternal beauty,
shouting out, "You are the great I Am,
the Alpha and Omega,
the beginning and the nd
of all that is, that was, and shall ever be,
from here to the ages to come
and through all eternity."

# Yesterday

When the whispering winds of yesterday blow along my path,
when the summer turns to fall,
and the trees are decorated with the fiery colors of glory;
they are cloaked with garments of majesty from on high.
When all nature cries out a new song of praise
this is the time in which I am mindful of You.
For You and only You are my King.
Yes, You and You only are my Savior.
You and You only are my Creator,
You and You only are my Redeemer.
I will praise You upon the sands of time for all eternity.
It is You who holds the candle of my heart,
set in its place to give me life.
For you are the Light of the World.
Only You can create within my very being
peace in the midst of the storm.
I do glory in You,
my Lord,
my God,
my Savior,
King of my heart.
I praise and magnify Your holy, precious name.
You, Lord Jesus, are the author and finisher of my life.
You are the keeper of all my yesterdays,
the Creator of all my tomorrows.
I surrender my spirit, soul, and body to You,
for You are my God from here to eternity past.

**Scriptures:**

But, God who is rich in mercy, because of His great
love with which He loved us, even when we were
dead in trespasses, made us alive together with

Christ (by grace you have been saved), and raised us up together in the heavenly places in Christ Jesus, that in the ages to come He might show the exceeding riches of His grace in his kindness toward us in Christ Jesus. For by faith you have been saved through faith, and that not of your selves; it is the gift of God, not of works, lest anyone should boast. For we are His workmanship, created in Christ Jesus for good works, which God prepared beforehand that we should walk in them.

Ephesians 2:4-10

# Forgive Me, Oh God!

Promises made, promises broken. How many times have you sinned against Jesus, your Lord God and Savior? As for me, I probably couldn't even count the number of times that His mercy, His grace, His blood, His loving hands out of the breeches of time and eternity rushed in like a flood to forgive me of my foolish ways.

His blood covers us past, future, and present. We do not go to hell if we commit a sin if we're saved, so why are we so quick to repent? The major reason is because we love Him. Who wants to hurt Jesus, our loving Savior? Not me. But unfortunately, sometimes I do sin and hurt Him. I take it very seriously when I hurt such a beautiful, loving God as my Jesus. There is an evil devil just waiting for the opportunity to find a way to come into our lives and destroy us. That avenue is sin. I love my God, my king, my loving Savior with all my heart.

We all fall down, but we thank God for His blood-stained robe of righteousness. He paid the price and took our place when we most assuredly deserved death a thousand times over. I am so thankful that He loves us and has offered the eternal gift of salvation to us. This free gift is for whosoever would ask. He is, was, and always shall be the way, the truth, and the life, forevermore.

**Scriptures:**

If we confess our sins, He is faithful and just to forgive us our sins and to cleanse us from all unrighteousness.

1 John 1:9

In Him, we have redemption through His blood, the forgiveness of sins, according to the riches of His grace.

Ephesians 1:7

# Promises Made, Promises Broken

Promises made,
promises broken.
Oh my Lord!
The words that I have spoken!
Idle words lost in a sea of nevermore.
As far as the east is from the west.
Oh my Lord,
my Joy,
my Peace,
how I thank You for Your loving hands,
Your loving heart of forgiveness.

Promises made,
promises broken.
Like the wind-swept ocean that washes away
all my sorrows of yesterday
to the outer reaches of time itself.

Promises made,
promises broken,
measures of our demise.
False treasures that we hunt for
when the true treasure rests within our hearts.
The King,
He lives,
He rests,
He breathes the breath of life,
He speaks to us with that quiet still voice of
love,
hope,
peace,
and joy,
speaking to us with His wisdom,
His truth,
His gentle touch of love.

Yes, oh my Lord!
Promises made,
promises broken.
Such is our demise.
We do things our way.
We speak the lies of yesterday
with the smile of false peace,
broken hearts upon the midnight blue.
Secrets of souls never spoken.
So fearful of love
to show we care.
Do we ever dare?
Feeling forsaken,
broken into,
bruised and betrayed,
taken for granted,
shielding our hearts from pain.

Promises made,
promises broken,
lonely survivors from the past.

Promises made,
promises broken.
You, Oh Lord, are the resurrection from the things I have spoken,
the lies of my past.
You, and only You Lord, are
my shield,
my refuge,
my hope,
my peace,
my joy,
the One who has forgiven me
of all of my
promises made,
my promises broken.
For You, and only You, are the King of my heart!
Amen!

# The Battle

Oh my Lord,
oh my God,
my king,
my peace,
my hope.
It is You that I praise.
It is You that I do glory in.
It is You that I do magnify
as I most sincerely lift up
Your holy and precious loving-kindness
unto the heavens above.
For You are Lord,
You are God,
You are my Savior,
my everything.
I cry out to You, my mentor of hope,
my teacher,
my counselor of love,
obedience,
and truth.
I try to do what is right.
I fall, I do what is wrong.
I try and I try.
I stumble.
Oh my king, I surrender!
I am nothing without You!
I stumble, I fall, I call out to You.
Forgive me!
Forgive me!
Forgive me!
For I am nothing without Your loving mercy and grace!

**Scriptures:**

For Your mercy is great above the heavens, and Your truth reaches to the clouds,
Be exalted, o God, above the heavens, and Your glory above all the earth:
That Your beloved may be delivered, save me with Your right hand, and hear me.

Psalm 108:4-6

# God Calls Out to Man

Are you crying out in the midst of the storms in your life? God is there. You may say, "I can't see Him. I can't feel Him." Why do you have to see Him? Why do you have to feel Him? You believe your employer when he promises to pay you for a good day's work. You believe man has landed on the moon. You believe that there are 24 hours in a day. You believe your teachers when they teach you that there are diamonds deep in the earth in Africa. Why do you not believe God when He tells you that He loves and cares for you.

There is a visible world and an invisible world. We have to believe God's word. God is the author over all there is, over all creation. When Jesus was on the earth, people would not even believe in Him, even though He could be seen, felt, and touched.

God is God, there is none other. Stop believing in the world only because you can see and touch something. Jesus is more real than you will ever know. He stepped out of heaven to appear, to live with us. He died for us, He cried for us, He shed His precious blood. His blood is our witness that there is hope! (1 John 5:8)

By His blood we are free from this world and all of its problems. Do you really want to live in a sin-infested world like this forever? Take His precious gift of life and simply and truly believe. He is waiting patiently for your prayers to be spoken, and to be answered with His mighty wisdom and power. He is Lord, He is God, He is Savior. He is Jesus, the King of kings, and Lord of lords, from here to eternity!

**Scriptures:**

Come to me all you who labor and are heavy laden, and I will give you rest.

Take my yoke upon you and learn from Me, for I am gentle and lowly in heart, and you will find rest for your souls.

For My yoke is easy and My burden is light.

Matthew 11:28-30

# Come to Me

Come to me, my child, for I am yours.
Come to me, my child, for you are Mine.
Come to me, my child, for
I will protect you.
I will comfort you.
I will heal you.
Come to me, my child, and fear not,
for I am with you when the storms of life crash in on you.
Yes, come to me. my child, for
I will love you.
I will give you peace.
I will give you joy.
Come to me, my little child, for I am your
Savior,
Your Lord,
Your God.
Come to me.
Come to me.
Come to me, my little one,
for I long to be with you in your pain.
I long to release you from the chains that bind you,
the burdens that choke you with despair.
Yes, come to me, my little child, my little lamb,
I am the good shepherd,
I will give you rest.
I will give you peace where there is pain.
I will give you hope where there is despair.
I will give you joy in the morning.
Where there is sorrow,
I will give you love.
Please, please,
come to me in the cool of the day, in the morning,
I will give you rest.

# I Am, I Was, and I Shall Forever be your God

I am, I said,
not of today,
not of tomorrow
and of yesterday,
but forevermore.
I am the creator of the cool breeze in the morning
when you awaken from your peaceful slumber at night.
I am the creator of the dew
as it kisses the plush green grass of a thousand hills
as far as the eye can see.
I am the creator of the mist of the ocean blue,
as the great and mighty waves of glory
crash up against the fortress high,
the rock of the ages past.
I am the One Who commands the clouds to go forth
and water the earth by the word of My power.

Now,
and even now,
My little one,
hear Me,
hear My heart,
hear Me as I cry out to you
with My tears of compassion,
of love,
and gentleness.
You were lost and now I have found you.
You were a prisoner and I have freed you.
You were destitute,
without a future,
only a distant call of yesterdays past.

But now hear what I have to say to you, My child,
as I plead My case.
All these things of old, of the distant past
have been changed.
They have been swept away by the passages,
the tides of time eternal,
for I am your champion.
I am your refuge, your high tower of hope,
and of peace.
I Am that I Am.
I am Alpha and Omega,
the beginning and the end of all things.
I am God Almighty,
your Creator Elohim.
I am Jehovah,
your King,
your Redeemer.
Hear me My child, My little one,
My most fondest of all creation,
you have been freed from the bondages
of sin and rebellion,
from the wicked task master,
that old dragon, Lucifer,
the eternal one of deceitfulness and lies.
Hear My cry.
Hear My plea.
You were bought with a price,
by My very blood,
by My body,
and by My spirit.
I say unto you once and for all,
this is a free gift, a gift of life eternal.
You and only you can accept or deny Me.
To choose me, is to choose life.
Choose and choose well,
for perilous times are right at the door.
I say unto you,

choose life, and I will love you forever.
I stand at the door of your heart as I cry out
unto the depth of your very soul and spirit.
I Am that I Am.
I call to you with all mercy and grace.
I love you My little one.
Please be mine, and I promise to love you,
forevermore, forevermore, forevermore,
until the end of eternity past!

# I Am That I Am

I am mindful of you, oh man.
I am yours and you are Mine.
I have bought you with a price,
by My very blood!
My witness, to your eternal peace!
I love you,
I care for you.
I am everything that you need.
I Am that I Am.
I am Alpha and Omega,
the first and the last,
your beginning and your end.
I am timeless outside of time.
I am the mighty One,
Your God,
the strong One.
I am your creator,
I am your redeemer,
I am your eternity,
from everlasting,
to everlasting!
Amen!

# My Child

My child,
am I not
the great I Am?
The one who stretches out My hand across the universe
with the word of My power to create the sky above,
the valley below?

Am I not
the creator of all that you see and hear?

Am I not
the author of your next breath,
the keeper of your heart eternal!
The gatekeeper of your spirit?

Am I not
the key to the very existence of your life?

Am I not
the protector of your spirit, soul, and body?

Am I not
the One who comes to you in the cool of the day,
in the midst of the storm?

Am I not
the One who cries out to you
in the valley of your pain and suffering
and calls out, "Peace be still?"

Am I not
always there for you?
Have I ever

deceived,
lied,
or abandoned you to this world and its fury?
Let us now reason together with this time of reckoning.
Why do you fear?
Why do you doubt?
Why do you not believe?

Trust Me, my child,
for I am yours and you are Mine.
For I Am that I Am.
I will always be there for you.
From here to eternity past!

# Our Life Never Forgotten

Our life is like a shadow,
as a whisper in the wind,
like the sands of time.
Only God knows our beginning and our end.
The tides rush in with all their fury,
waves crashing the rocks of splendor proclaiming,
"I am here."
Then as the autumn winds gently push
the leaves of summer past,
the leaves are gently swept up
and thrown away into a place
never to be seen again.
So is our life like a shadow,
a whisper in the wind,
the tides of all of our glory.
All our hopes, dreams of yesterday past,
have now passed away,
the leaves of eternity past.
As a book without a cover,
author unknown,
thrown into the sea of nevermore.
First we live, then we die.
The world pushes the memories of
who and what we were,
into the vast oceans of lost treasures,
timeless treasures of infinity
and thoughts without end.
Yes, here we are,
we were,
the creation eternal,
ones of God eternal and all his glory.
Forgotten!
Forgotten!
Forevermore
into the days of eternity forgotten.

Then comes forth a mighty voice of thunder,
a flash of lightening
proclaiming,
"Who do you think you are, little man,
speaking for Me,
saying that you are forgotten?
I proclaim,
I have washed you with My atoning blood
of glory,
might,
and power.
You, my little one of splendor and grace,
mercy and compassion,
you are Mine.
You are My child.
You are My fondest creation.
Do you not understand?
Do you not perceive the fact that when you fall asleep,
awaken,
come to me,
then and only then,
you have just started to live.
This I declare, this I speak,
you will never be forgotten.
You will never be thrown into the sea of nevermore,
for I, and I alone, will never let go of your hand!
You will never be out of My eternal reach and power.
I am your Lord, I am your God, I am your Creator,
I am your Redeemer
for all times throughout all eternity.
Forevermore,
forevermore,
forevermore.
I will never forget you,
nor will I, your God of all that is, that was, or ever shall be.
ever let go of your hand!"

# The Voice

I am the One
you are searching for.
I am the One
that will give you rest.

I am the One
You are searching for.
I will give you peace.

I am the One
You are searching for
I will give you joy in the morning.

I am the One
You are searching for.
I have given you the stars at night,
the moon above,
my glory all around.

I have given you the sun to keep you warm
during the cold winter days
when the problems of this life
put chains of distress and frustration all about you,
chains of hopelessness and despair.
I Am that I Am.
There is nothing too hard for Me,
for I am the Lord your God
the great and the mighty One
The Holy One of God.

Am I not the Creator of all that is and ever will be?
Am I not your Redeemer?
Come to me!

Come to me!
Oh come to me
in your time of trouble!

I will rescue you from your enemies,
from the snares of the wicked ones of this world.
I will give you rest.
I will give you hope.
I will strengthen you in the midst of the storm.
I am the quiet, still rains of
peace,
hope,
love,
joy,
life eternal.

I am your salvation.
I am the way,
the truth,
and the life.
There is no other way than My way.
Do not be fooled by the world and what it has to offer.
The world's ways will deceive you
with false truth and false beauty
and will lead you in the end to your total destruction.

I am the One
you are searching for.
I am yours.

I am the One
you are searching for.
You are Mine.

I am the One
you are searching for.
I am the true loving God of your salvation,
your very life.

Follow me, for once again I speak
from My heart to your heart
I am the way,
the truth,
and the life
from here to eternity past!

# I Am Here for You

I am here for you.

I Am that I Am.

I am
your love in the midst of turmoil.

I am
your joy in the midst of the pain and suffering.

I am
your peace in the midst of the storm.

I am
your hope in the midst of destruction.

I am
the omnipotent One, all-powerful.

I am
the omnipresent One,
always present,
always there for you.

I am
the omniscient One,
all knowing, all seeing.

I am
life and I am love in the midst of the storm,
For I am your God!

**Scriptures:**

Now when the tempter came to Him, he said, "If you are the Son of God, command that these stones become bread."

But He answered and said, "it is written, man shall not live by bread alone, but by every word that proceeds from the mouth of God."

Matthew 4:3-4

# The Great Deception

The treacherous plans of the enemy, that old dragon, has deceived man many times over. He deceives, he lies, he discredits God's holy Word . He loves to twist the scriptures to confuse and cause godly men to fall away by false doctrine. Beware of the blinders the enemy places upon Christians and the nonbelievers. Beware, for he knows the Word better than you ever will.

It is time for one and all Christians to believe, speak, and proclaim the holy, powerful, precious, Word of God. It's time to stand up to be a witness. It's time to honor God and all His glory. You may say to me, "Who do you think you are, condemning me with your bold words?" My friend, God has spoken already, "I proclaim, I am One calling to you in the wilderness, heart to heart, life to life." This is the day of your salvation. This is the day of your reckoning with God Almighty. This is the day that your one and only God is calling out to you with the very blood He shed just for you on calvary. Every drop of blood He shed has a name engraved upon it. Are you going to be the one that throws away this precious gift of life with the mighty, loving, caring, Jesus Christ, the Son of the living God? It's time to look at the Word of God one more time. Could God be right and the false prophets be wrong with their words of deceit and confusion? Think about it. You'll be glad you did. Is this book speaking to your heart? Surrender! It's time to give your life to Jesus once and for all. No more games.

**Scriptures:**

And as it is appointed for men to die once, but after this the judgement,
So Christ was offered once to bear the sins of many. To those who eagerly wait for Him He will appear a second time, apart from sin, for salvation.

Hebrews 9:27-28

# Death Rides a Horse

Death rides a horse,
a horse of many colors.
Which horse will you be riding
when your time has come to depart this earth?
If you ride with Jesus Christ, the Son of the living God,
you will ride into clouds of glory
and see the colors of
righteousness,
peace,
joy,
victory,
and salvation
by His very blood.
You will be sheltered and comforted
by the wings of angels.
So tell me.
Tell me true.
Will you ride the horse of the enemy,
the colors of
death,
hell,
and the grave?
Will you be within and all about,
covered with the colors of
destruction,
plague,
disease,
and total damnation from here to eternity?
Now heed my warning as I call out to you,
which horse will you choose to ride?
The horse that rides to the final destination
of victory and peace everlasting
in the precious arms of Jesus,

or the horse of
death,
hell,
and the grave,
total destruction
where the canker worms are never satisfied
by the abundance of flesh they consume.
So now let us reason together.
Tell me.
Tell me true.
Which horse will you ride
when it's your time to depart this earth?
It's really up to you.
Choose, and choose well.
As for me and my house,
we choose Jesus Christ,
the Son of the Living God.

# I Tried to Tell Him, Lord

I tried to tell him, Lord,
of Your blood,
Your mercy,
Your grace,
Your gift of salvation.
I tried to tell him, Lord,
of Your unfailing love.
He told me,
"I'm okay,
I'm a good person,
I do good things,
I'm really okay,
I'm fine."
I tried to tell him, Lord,
of Your blood,
Your mercy,
Your grace,
Your gift of salvation.
I tried to tell him You are
the Way,
the Truth,
and the Life.
That You are Jesus Christ, the Son of the living God,
the only way to the Father.
The only way is through You
and Your precious blood to receive salvation.
My dearest King,
my heart aches,
my soul cries.
My spirit prays,
hopes,
pleads
for a man who spoke the words of

denial,
blindness,
and destruction.
Lord, I didn't even know his name.
Lord, what else can I do?
I spoke Your word.
I proclaimed you were
the Way,
the Truth,
the Life,
the only way to heaven.
I did my best, Lord.
I gave my all, to be Your witness.
Tell me, tell me true.
Do you know this man, the one who spoke
the words of deception from the enemy
out of denial,
blindness,
and destruction?
The Lord, He spoke.
He comforted me.
He said,
"Give me his heart, Son,
and I'll take care of the rest."

# I Walk Away

My Lord,
I will not walk with You,
I will not talk with You,
I will not be with You anymore,
For You have broken my heart.
I am not Yours,
And You are not mine.
Leave me alone.
Let me go.

My dearest loving daughter,
do you not know?
Have you not heard
that I am the keeper of Your heart?
Do you not know that I hold the key to your very soul?
Have you forgotten that you are My creation?
I adopted you.
I accepted you as My very own.
My daughter,
My child,
My little princess,
do you not know the affection I have for you
when you sleep?
I assign angels to watch over you.
I stand at your bedside in awe of your very next breath.
Do you truly reject me and push me away?
What have I done?
Are you sure that the enemy,
that old serpent, the devil,
has not spawned thoughts of deception in your mind?
Are you sure you want to push Me away?
Have you forgotten that you were bought with a price
by My very blood?

I cannot let you go!
I will not let you go!
I love you too much.
Part of you is in Me
and part of Me is in you.
How can I reject, deny Myself?
My final answer is this.
I love you,
I need you,
I will not violate My word.
I am yours,
and you are Mine,
forevermore,
until the very last breath of eternity past.
I love you.
I love you.
I love you.
and that, My child,
is My final, ending statement,
sealed with my blood,
and my very life!

# Tears of Time Eternal

Vanity, oh vanity, little man.
Do you not know by now looking back
through the tears of time
and all the failures of mankind,
that you are not God?
God is God, there is none other.
There is a place in your heart made for God,
and only God.

Vanity, oh vanity, little man.
God the Creator, Elohim,
the maker of heaven and sky, space and time
calls out to you!
You believe, you speak, "there is no God."
Yet you worship the sun, the moon, and the stars,
the almighty dollar.
Now that you are not fulfilled with that life, you hypocrite,
you scheme a different plan.
You set yourself up and you say, "I am God."
You fool of fools,
do you not know?
Have you not heard of
the greatness,
the mighty power of the Lord,
the mercy, the grace, the kindness
of love in his heart for you?
He shed His precious blood for you.
Do not take His loving compassion as weakness.
His power is as vast and marvelous,
as the east is from the west.

Vanity, oh vanity, little man
of deception, and lies.

You say there is no God.
Does this make it so?
God the Redeemer, Jehovah true,
He pleads for your heart to come to Him.

Vanity, oh vanity, little man
of pride and arrogance.
Do you not know that you are nothing
without Jesus Christ,
the Son of the living God,
the Mighty One,
the Holy One,
the Creator,
Redeemer,
the mighty Lion of Judah?
Oh little man of vanity, strife, deception, and lies,
did you hang the moon, set the stars in place,
align, create, build the universe?

Vanity, oh vanity, little man.
Who are you to say there is no God?
The tears of time have proven you wrong.
He is God!
He is Alpha and Omega,
your beginning, and your end!
Choose, and choose well, oh little man of vanity.
Will you choose
death,
hell
and the grave,
or will you choose Jesus Christ
the Son of the Living God,
life eternal?
Either way, if you choose Jesus,
you will have life eternal.
If you do not choose, you have chosen the enemy.
There is a real hell, as well as a real heaven.

Choose Jesus before it's too late.
You know you're running out of time.
Heaven, hell, and all eternity,
will be awaiting your answer!
Amen!
Forevermore!
Forevermore!
Forevermore!
Unto the end of eternity past!!!

# The Storm Is Coming

The storm is coming.
Do you not see it?
The storm is coming.
Do you not hear it?
The storm is coming.
Do you not perceive it?
Do you not know the call of
the Lord God almighty Elohim,
the creator of your very being?
Do you not see the calling upon your life?
Do you not perceive the right hand of righteousness
guiding you to make ready
for the kingdom of God?
Do you not know that upon this very moment in time
Jehovah our redeemer,
the great I Am,
has rearranged the whole entire universe
for you to read and understand the words
which I have penned for your heart to accept?
The storm is coming.
It is now your appointed time in this earth to decide.
Will your decision be
death,
hell,
and the grave with the enemy,
or do you choose Jesus Christ, the Son of the living God,
the author of
righteousness,
peace,
joy,
and salvation?
The storm is coming.
Choose, and choose well.

There is still time.
Jesus shed His blood for you,
He paid the price.
The decision is yours.
Choose and choose well,
for your choice will last from here to eternity
and beyond!

# God's Merciful Salvation

In all the wars fought, there have been many heroes that came forth throughout the ages -- wars of the flesh for kingdoms present and kingdoms past and the spiritual wars for our eternal souls. David, Sampson and Daniel, to name a few of these heros.

Out of all the warriors of the past, present, and future is King Jesus Christ, the merciful, saving, caring One, Who stepped out of heaven into the earth to save us from ourselves and from death, hell, and the grave. If not for our loving Savior, where would we be? Jesus took on the world. He won the victory. He took our place by living a sinless life. By His very blood, He won back whosoever would come to Him. If not for the King of kings, the Lord of lords, where would we be?

I believe in my loving King of glory. The world tells me I'm a fool to believe in fairy tales. I proclaim that the world and all of its many voices of false doctrine and deceit are the fools. In the Word of God, it declares prideful men to be the fools.

—— My God of mercy, love, and peace is always loving, always caring, always ready to accept us right where we are. I invite you one and all to not search for the religious Jesus, but the real Jesus who will love you unconditionally, unlike the religious system that shoots their wounded instead of loving them back to health.

**Scriptures:**

"Come now, let us reason together," Says the Lord, "Though your sins are like scarlet, They shall be white as snow; Though they are red like crimson, They shall be as wool.

If you are willing and obedient, You shall eat the
good of the land;
   But if you refuse and rebel, You shall be devoured
by the sword"; For the mouth of the lord has spoken.

Isaiah 1:18-20

# Alone

Alone, alone, I sailed.
Alone, alone, I sailed the salty sea.
Alone, alone, I sailed the salty seas of yesterdays past
looking up into the moonlit sky as beams of pale-lit light
danced upon the silent waters of the evening blue.
Now, and even now, the clouds of God's holy glory
captured and illuminated the moonlight
and focused it directly into my eyes.
I beheld His glory,
His majesty,
His handiwork
in the sky above,
the earth below.
Mountains high,
valleys low,
seemed to applaud His creative power
as the dawn's early light
pierced through the rainbow-colored clouds
of the early morn.
Without saying a word,
God almighty,
Elohim,
the master potter,
spoke to me volumes of
His mercy,
His grace,
love,
hope,
and peace.
God spoke to me and had me to recall
when I was but a young lad of six years old
in a Sunday morning service.
He reminded me to recall the song,

"Jesus Loves Me."
He also reminded me of the blood,
the precious blood of Jesus.
Now within a moment's notice
I finally understood the message of
hope,
love,
salvation,
and His loving hands,
the gift of eternal life.
Upon this very night
I surrendered,
I yielded,
I gave my heart to Jesus Christ,
the Son of the living God,
my Savior,
my King.
He is the very reason I live and I breathe.
Now as I sail upon the mighty waters,
the waves of glory,
the salty sea of beauty,
life abounding,
I sail with the King of glory,
The keeper of my heart,
the author of my next breath,
the master potter of all of my tomorrows,
until the dawn of eternities past shall fade away
into the tides of time eternal forevermore!
Amen!

# A Moment from Midnight

A moment from midnight
On a snowy, snowy night,
A night of pain,
A night of sorrow,
A night of confusion,
I walked the icy streets of yesterday.
I cried the tears of my past.

A moment before midnight
On a snowy, snowy night,
I walked alone with a broken heart,
searching for
peace,
joy,
and a reason to live!

Just one moment from midnight
on a snowy, snowy night,
on an icy walk of loneliness and shame,
You touched my heart,
You broke the chains,
You spoke my name,
You gave me peace,
You shed Your blood,
You set me free!

Yes, on a snowy, snowy night,
One moment before midnight,
You gave me life eternal,
Your mercy,
Your grace,
Your love,
Your gentleness,
Your kindness.

A moment before midnight
On a snowy, snowy night,
I walked into the
compassionate,
loving,
caring,
saving arms of my Jesus Christ
the Son of the living God.

A moment before midnight
On a snowy, snowy night,
I walked the icy streets
together,
together,
as a citizen of heaven,
A child of the Most High God,
Forevermore!
Forevermore!
Forevermore,
unto the eternal love, and rest of Jesus Christ my King!

Now as I live and I do breathe,
I will proclaim God's good news,
the gospel unto the very day that I shall die!

# A Simple Man's Prayer

Father God, I am but a simple man,
a man of few talents.
I am not a man that anyone would pick out in a crowd
as being special.
I am but a carpenter's son
from the Blue Ridge Mountains of West Kentucky.
I have heard the preacher man several times
call out to my heart
But I never walked the aisle to receive salvation.
I've heard so many times of
Your love,
Your gentleness,
Your mercy,
Your grace,
Your blood,
Your sacrifice.
I've heard that you're the one who heals the brokenhearted.
Well Lord, I'm the one.
I'm the one with the broken heart.
I'm tired of sin.
I'm tired of my life.
I'm tired of this guilt,
this weight upon my shoulders.
Lord God, will you help?
Will You heal this broken heart?
Will You receive this old man,
this simple man of despair?
Lord, if you're willing, then here am I oh Lord.
I'm yours.
Just a simple man from the Blue Ridge Mountains
of West Kentucky.

# Love Is God, God Is Love

Love is God.
God is love.
You cannot separate the two.
God stepped out of heaven into this earth
with all compassion
to rescue us from
self-destruction,
pain,
and the sorrows of this world.

Love is God.
God is love.
You cannot separate the two.
Jesus Christ, the Son of the living God,
stepped out of heaven,
laid aside his heavenly robe of power and authority
to proclaim the gospel of peace.

Love is God.
God is love.
You cannot separate the two.
Jesus, the mighty One,
the Holy One of
peace,
mercy,
and grace,
set aside His mighty powers to rescue us
from
death,
hell,
and the grave.

Love is God.
God is love.
You cannot separate the two.
Jesus,
my Lord,
my Savior,
my king,
my holy sacrifice,
offered himself as the Lamb for the slaughter,
the eternal sacrifice once and for all
so that we may have life and peace,
in abundance forever.

Love is God.
God is love.
You cannot separate the two.
By His own power of choice
He loved us unto death.
He allowed the enemy and mankind
to break His body,
as He spilled His life's blood to kiss the ground
with His gift of life, with all compassion
for all that would call out His holy, holy, name.

Love is God.
God is love.
You cannot separate the two.
Jesus Christ, the Son of the living God,
great and mighty King of glory
paid the price for all of our sins.
Upon the third day, He arose from the dead
by the power of the Holy Spirit
with a mighty sound of thunder,
lightening in the sky above,
and from within the tomb as the earth shook,
even as to say,

"You are Lord, you are God,
you are the King over all creation, of all there is,
all there was, or ever shall be."

Love is God, God is love.
You cannot separate the two.
Have you by the grace of God
accepted Jesus Christ's love and sacrifice today?
Well, He is waiting with all compassion today
to accept you into His arms
of
love,
mercy,
and grace.

# Heaven-Bound Forevermore!

Day by day, night by night, the glory of God almighty is all around us. He surrounds us with His gentle hands of love, mercy, and grace eternal. He is there in times of trouble. He is there in times of peace. He is there! He is there! He is there with you always. Do you not perceive it? He is the king of your heart. Rejoice, oh my friends, my loving brothers and sisters! For He is eternal. He is love. He is your peace in the midst of the storm. He is yours and you are His.

Jesus tells us in his Word, "In the world you will have tribulation; but be of good cheer, I have overcome the world" (John 16:33). This is for you - the one who has lost a child, brother, sister, wife, husband, parent, friend, to death. Oh death, where oh where is your sting? To be absent from the body is to be present with the Lord. If we stand under the umbrella, the kingdom of God, then what do we have to fear? The rain may fall, the winds may blow, but we are protected by His loving, caring hands of mercy, grace, eternal peace.

Remember always, no matter what problems we have in this life, Jesus is there. He lives inside of us if we are His. We were bought with a price. He paid the price to reclaim us. By His precious blood, His love, His bodily sacrifice, Jesus willingly, lovingly, paid the ransom. We are, by His sacrifice of His life, no longer our own. I don't know about you, but I do not want to be my own, for I fall, I stumble, I faint without the leading of His loving nail-pierced hands of glory. You see, He is the King of Glory. It is because of His remembrance of me that I do live and breathe. He is the keeper of my heart and life. I proclaim, "If not to live for Him, then it's time for me to die."

Without Jesus in your life, what is there to live for? Your next paycheck? Your next bill? Your next birthday? I ask you truly, what is there to live for if not to live for Him?

I surrender! I surrender my heart, my mind, my body, soul and spirit over to you, my loving Jesus.

**Scriptures:**

Oh come, let us sing to the Lord! Let us shout joyfully to the rock of our salvation.

Psalm 95: 1

For you were bought at a price; therefore glorify God in your body and in your spirit, which are God's.

1 Corinthians 6:20

Jesus said to her, "I am the resurrection and the life. He who believes in me, though he may die, he shall live."
"And whoever lives and believes in me shall never die. Do you believe this?"

John 11:25-26

Let not your heart be troubled; you believe in God, believe also in me.

John 14:1

Greater love has no one than this, than to lay down one's life for his friends.

John 15:13

You are worthy, O Lord, To receive glory and honor and power; For You created all things, And by Your will they exist and were created.

Revelation 4:11

And every creature which is in heaven and on the earth and under the earth and such as are in the sea, and all that are in them, I heard saying:

"Blessing and honor and glory and power Be to Him who sits on the throne, And to the Lamb, forever and ever!"

Revelation 5:13

# I'm Finally Home

I did not know this would be my last day to live.
I prayed.
I praised.
I worshipped God.
I read His Word.
I thanked Him for the new day.

I did not know this would be my last day to live.
I marveled at the handiwork,
the painting on the canvas of the sky.
The beauty of the sunset upon high,
with its beautiful colors all around me.
I was awestruck with the beautiful meadow below,
with the colors of peace and tranquility,
and from the top of this magnificent
snow-covered mountaintop,
I beheld the beauty of His glory and His majesty.

I did not know this would be my last day to live.
I went to work doing the normal routines of the day.
I had a problem here and there
just like anybody else on the job.
But this day was special.
You see, I died that day.
I did not cry.
I was not in anguish or pain,
for I beheld the glory of the Lord my God all around me.
The angels said to me,
"It's time to go home."
I was then escorted to the throne room of God.
I could not contain myself.
I exploded with the joy of the Lord!
I felt such love that I cried the tears

of gladness and thanksgiving!
I laughed, I cried, I rejoiced,
I was finally home!
Home, where I knew I belonged.
All around me the saints of God almighty,
the elders, the angels were singing,
"Worthy is the lamb who was slain,
to receive power and wealth and wisdom and strength and honor and
glory and praise."*
All around the throne there were flashes of lightning,
rumblings and peals of thunder.
And there I saw Him -
my Lord, my God, my Savior, my king,
the Lion of Judah, the great I Am,
my everything, my loving Jesus,
as He walked towards me by the sea of glass, clear as crystal,
and He spoke these words to me,
"Well done, my good and faithful servant.
Now enter into the joy of the Lord,
the inheritance of your Lord God."

I did not know this would be my last day to live.
Thank you, my Lord
that I chose you to be my King of Kings and Lord of Lords
and that You chose me
to be Your child, Your bride, Your little one
For all eternity and beyond!


* Revelation 5:12

# The Song Is Over

The song is over.
My life has expired.
I have fought the good fight,
now the race has been won.
Yes, the song is over.
It's time to rejoice in the sweet by and by,
in the presence of the King.
The song is over,
a new life I begin.
So do not weep,
do not cry for me.
I am indeed a child of the Most High God.
Now sing with me a song of love,
sing with me a song of hope,
sing with me a song of peace forevermore.
No, do not mourn for me,
do not weep,
do not cry for me,
for I have been carried by the wings of angels
into the loving arms of my God, and your God.
Jesus Christ, the Son of the living God.

# Time to Go

I am not long for this world.
My life is spent.
My life is like a vapor,
like a mist reaching out
into the passages of time and space.
I am not long for this world.
Do not weep for me.
The dew will still kiss the ground in the morning.
The birds will still sing their songs of praise
to the God of heaven above.
I am not long for this world.
Do not weep for me.
Know that I have passed on into the passages of time
into the loving, caring arms of my Lord Jesus Christ,
my God, my Savior, the One Who died for me,
the One Who cried for me,
the One Who went through the pain of the ages,
pouring out His last drop of blood
to kiss the ground with the tears of salvation
from here to eternity past.
So do not cry for me.
Do not mourn for me,
for I rest in the glory of the Lord my God.
All of heaven surrounds me
as I kneel and bow before
the majestic,
loving,
caring,
Jesus Christ,
the Lion of Judah,
the Rose of Sharon,
the Prince of Peace.
Forevermore,
forevermore,
forevermore!

# When this Life Is Over

When this life is over,
when I have flown away to the arms of
my Lord,
my God,
my Savior,
as I have rested in the wings of the angels.
When I have run the race,
finished the good fight,
the fight of faith,
I will go in the slumber of peace, safety, protection,
knowing that I have been victorious
within the battles and the conquests of this world,
for I have been covered by the holy sacrifice,
the precious blood of Jesus Christ,
the Son of the Living God,
the Alpha and Omega,
the Beginning and the End,
the author and finisher of my life.
I speak this encouragement to you
my friend,
my brother in Jesus Christ,
the anointed one of God.
Do not weep for me.
Do not cry.
Do not be sad.
For I have been covered by
the blood of the Lamb,
the Lion of Judah,
the Rose of Sharon,
the author of my life.
My salvation,
my hope,
my peace,

my joy.
No, my wife,
my love,
my friend,
my eternal joint partner,
love of my life,
do not weep for me,
do not cry,
for I will be waiting for you
on the other side of the midnight blue
resting in the arms of my God and your God.

# Hell Bound!

I say to you, my friend, this writing is not to hurt you but to love you; to cause you to open your eyes to see that King Jesus does live and breathe.

He is real. He is Lord. He is God. He is Savior. He and He alone is life - the lover of your spirit, soul, and body, the creator of your very being. He is not a fairy tale, a story to help you to go to sleep at night. He is not a fabrication of man's lies and deceit on the evening news. Stop listening to the lies of the enemy and the world. You already know the truth. The battlefield is in your mind. That is where the enemy plays his little games as he spawns his plans for you to reject Jesus Christ. Jesus Christ, the Son of the Living God died for you, He cried for you.

Upon this very moment in time He is making a final attempt to touch your sin-torn heart to say, "I love you. I care for you. I am yours. Will you be mine? I have done all I can to save you from your sins. Your greatest sin is rejecting me. I have already payed the price for you. Please don't throw away my free gift to you. I have shed My blood for you. I have been the lamb for the slaughter for you and you alone. Do you not hear My blood even now as it calls out your name, heart to heart, life to life, spirit to spirit? You are lost. I have left the other sheep to find you. Do you truly believe you are reading this book by accident? I have rearranged all heaven and earth, time and space to call you lovingly, caringly. Little one, come home! I miss you, please come home! I love you! I need you! Please come to me before it's too late. I say, I speak, I proclaim, 'All heaven and earth, the angels in and all around await your answer.'"

**Scriptures:**

And as it is appointed for men to die once, but after this the judgement, once to live then to die the judgement.

So Christ was offered once to bear the sins of many. To those who eagerly wait for Him He will appear a second time, apart from sin, for salvation.

Hebrews 9:27,28

is a faithful saying, worthy of all acceptation, that Christ Jesus came into the world to save sinners.

I Timothy 1:15

For all have sinned and come short of the glory of God.

Romans 3:23

As it is written there is none righteous no not one.

Romans 3:10

He who hears you hears Me, he who rejects you rejects Me, and he who rejects Me rejects Him who sent Me.

Luke 10:16

If the world hates you, you know that it hated Me before it hated you. If you were of the world, the world would love its own. Yet because you are not of the world, but I choose you out of the world, therefore the world hates you. Remember that the word that I said to you, A servant is not greater than his master. If they persecuted me, they will also persecute you. If they kept My word, they will keep yours also. But all these things they will do to you for My name's sake, because they do not know Him who sent Me, If I had not come and spoken to them. They would have no sin, but now they have no excuse for their sin. He who hates Me hates My Father also.

John 15:18-23

I am the vine, you are the branches. He who abides in Me, and I in him, bears much fruit; for without Me you can do nothing.

John 15:5

# My Last Day

I did not know this would be my last day to live.
I drank.
I smoked.
I told the latest dirty joke.
I did not know this would be my last day to live.
I laughed in the bar with all of my buddies
as we made fun at the newest preacher man on TV.
We cussed.
We made fun of Jesus and that blood.
The preacher man,
he kept on sayin',
"Surrender your life, your heart to Jesus,
it's not too late."
I did not know this would be my last day to live.
Me and the boys, we kept on having fun,
poking fun at the preacher man on the TV.
He kept on talkin' about that blood and heaven.
He kept on sayin,
"Surrender your life, your heart to Jesus,
it's not too late."
I did not know this would be my last day to live.
I said goodbye to the fellows.
I had too much to drink that night.
Drunk as a skunk, I started driving home.
The rain poured down.
I couldn't see a thing.
There was a curve.
I missed the turn.
I crashed down the mountainside,
screaming in fear and panic.
I did not know this would be my last day to live.
As I looked at my body layin' there,
I cried out to God,

"Please help me. Please, please, save me."
It was too late!
Now all that awaited me was death, hell, and the grave.
Then, demons from hell escorted me to my own personal pit,
made for me, and me alone.
My skin, it burned,
it rotted,
it kept on decaying as the years rolled by.
The pain,
the sorrow,
the thoughts of the past,
all the harm that I had done to others
kept on coming back to my mind.
I cried out to God over and over again with no answer
until I finally remembered the preacher man on TV
as he kept on sayin',
"Surrender your life, your heart to Jesus,
i'ts not too late."
Tell me, tell me true,
are you the one destined to go to hell
of your own accord?
Are you the one who is rejecting the loving, caring blood, the witness
of truth eternal?

Are you the one rejecting the precious holy name of Jesus.
Well, I'm the preacher man, calling out to you
with all my heart
as I keep on sayin,
"Surrender your life, your heart to Jesus,
it's not too late,
...or is it?"

# I Surrender to You!

I surrendered my life to Jesus as a young boy. I still remember even as a very young boy the feeling I had. Upon that very moment in time, my heart was filled with joy and peace. I told Jesus and my parents that I was going to be the best boy in the whole wide world. I truly meant it at the time. Things in my life changed. I went to church here and there with friends. Then I became increasingly absent from church. But before I left for the Navy, I started going back to church with a girlfriend who loved God very much.

When I finally departed to go into the Navy, I talked to people about Jesus, but they would make fun of me. I didn't understand. All kinds of different things happened to me. I thought God was kicking me in the teeth over and over again. I didn't know it was the enemy deceiving me and causing all the trouble in my life. I was deeply offended with God. I told Him, "God, if this is the way you are going to treat me, then just forget it!" I ran away from home, from my God.

Hear me one and all - it says in the Word of God, "My people are destroyed for lack of knowledge." (Hosea 4:6) I warn you strongly, study and know the Word of God. I was deceived. I did all kinds of sin. I was an idiot. My dad told me, "Son, you've been going up fool's hill. Go back to God and he will help you get back to where you belong."

Four years later, I finally wised up and surrendered and came back to God. I have never forgotten that lesson. Don't learn the hard way. Study the Word and know that the true loving God operates in your life with love, not beatings and evil words of hatred. His message to you is always the same: "I love you."

**Scriptures:**

If we confess our sins, He is faithful and just to forgive our sins and to cleanse us from all unrighteousness.

1 John 1:9

# Here Am I, Oh Lord

Here am I, oh Lord.
I am Your servant.
Here am I, oh Lord.
I am Yours to command.
Here am I, oh Lord.
I have surrendered
my very life,
soul,
and spirit,
humbly and respectfully over to You,
You and only You.
I have taken up my cup of salvation
as I called upon the name of the Lord.
I call upon Your holy, precious name.
I know that You have heard my cry.
I will offer up to You the sacrifice of thanksgiving,
the cup of worship,
the cry of surrender,
the dedication of obedience,
from my heart to Your heart.
I am mindful of You oh Lord, God, and Savior.
For You are merciful.
You are kind.
You have kissed my life
with the gift of Your grace and mercy.
You have poured out the gift of
peace,
hope,
and joy
by the brokenness of Your heart,
the spilling of Your precious, holy blood
as it kissed the ground,
as it cried out to the heavens above,

the valleys below,
"It is finished,
it is finished,
it is finished."
From this time forward
I am Yours!
I am Yours!
I am Yours!
Forevermore and beyond!
Amen!

# I Love You, Lord

I love
the stars up above.

I love
the way the wind blows the wavering green leaves of spring.

I love
gardens filled with lush greenery
which seems to sing out in laughter upon the whispering wind.

I love
the sparkling waves upon the reaches of the seashore
so graceful.

I love
the sunset,
which brings forth the awakening of life and its beauty.

I love
the moon which beams down to show me the way of life,
guiding me into the future, all my tomorrows yet unseen.

I love
the simple way the brooks flow upon the rocks
and rush past, whispering a song of beauty.

I love
the mountains so high with peaks that reach upon the very essence
of the heavens.

Yes, I love
all of these things in life,
for you, oh Lord my God,are

the author of all my tomorrows,
the keeper of my heart.
The creator of my very life.

I live because You speak my name
in the midst of the storms of my very life.
I live,
I love and breathe,
because your light shines in and through me
unto eternity past and beyond!
Amen!

# Listen

Listen to the voice of My heart
as it cries out to you.
Deep to deep,
life to life,
as the sun goes down,
the stars come out,
to sing a song of
peace,
love
and serenity.
You are Lord,
You are God,
You are the King.
As the night goes on
the moon glides upon the midnight blue
proclaiming that You are the great I Am of all creation.
From everlasting
to everlasting.
The wind, it blows,
the trees, they sway back and forth,
as praise comes forth
from the very depths of His creation
proclaiming You, and You alone
are the author and finisher
for the glory of all creation!

# My Days Are in Your Hands

What are the dreams of a young man's heart,
but the leading of his footsteps
to righteousness, peace, and joy
by the Lord of Glory?
I speak, I say, I proclaim,
"My days are in Your hands, oh Lord God Almighty."
It is you that I will follow,
the Good Shepherd,
the God of my fathers, and their fathers before them.
I will not follow a stranger's voice.
I will forever throughout all eternity
proclaim my loyalties to You, my King.
I am yours!
I am yours!
I am yours,
Bought with a price by the sacrifice of Your body,
by the shedding of Your precious blood.
With all my strength, all my might
I have declared, proclaimed, shared,
and shouted from the rooftops,
"Jesus Christ is Lord!"
This name I share with You is to be praised
throughout the breachless sands of time eternal.
I am your servant, oh God.
Upon bended knee,
my head bowed in honor and reverence of You and only You
have I declared You to be king and ruler over me
and all who live under my roof.

# Jesus Christ, Our Precious Gift!

There was a baby, a very special baby. His life was foretold even before He was born. He was called by many names: Wonderful, Counselor, Mighty God, Everlasting Father, the Prince of Peace. He was, is, and always shall be the holy sacrifice. The lamb for the slaughter. The mighty One of God. He grew up from a small baby into the greatest man ever born. His name is Jesus. He was man and God at the same time. He stepped out of heaven to Earth. He came as a bond-servant. He shed His very blood, gave up his life to save us. Because of His sacrifice, we are free indeed.

**Scriptures:**

For unto us a Child is born, unto us a Son is given; and the government will be upon His shoulder. And His name will be called Wonderful, Counselor, Mighty God, Everlasting Father, Prince of Peace.

Of the increase of His government and peace there will be no end, upon the throne of David and over His kingdom, to order it and establish it with judgement and justice. From that time forward, even forever. The zeal of the Lord of hosts will perform this.

Isaiah 9:6-7

And behold, you will conceive in your womb and bring forth a Son, and shall call His name Jesus.

He will be great, and will be called the Son of the Highest; and the Lord God will give Him the throne of His father David.

And he will reign over the house of Jacob forever, and of His kingdom there will be no end.

Luke 1:31-33

# To Us a Child Is Born

On a starry, starry, night
down a dusty, dusty, road
that leads to Bethlehem, the town of David.
To us a Child is born.
A Child of peace,
a Child of love,
a Child of hope,
a Child of glory,
a Child of life eternal,
the Savior of the world.
The Great and the Mighty One
Who would deliver us from our sins
by the power of His blood eternal.

Yes, once and for all
on a starry, starry, night;
on a dusty, dusty, road;
there is a Child,
the Son,
the Savior,
Jesus Christ, the Son of the living God.

Yes, on a starry, starry, night,
on a dusty, dusty, road
the prophets of old spoke of
a Child of glory,
a Child of authority
through the mighty loving, caring, power of the Holy Spirit.

Yes, on a starry, starry, night,
on a dusty, dusty, road
that leads to the deliverance of the captives,
lays in a manger

the Messenger of salvation,
the Messenger of joy,
the Messenger of peace,
the Messenger from God Almighty Himself.
He will be called,
Wonderful,
Counselor,
Mighty God,
Everlasting Father,
Prince of Peace.
Of the increase of His government and peace
there will be no end.
He will reign on David's throne
and over his kingdom,
establishing and upholding it
with justice and righteousness
from that time on and forever.
The King of Glory stepped out of heaven,
lowering Himself as a servant for all mankind
to suffer the pains of our sin
to win us back to Himself once and for all.
Thank you, my loving King Jesus
for all that You have done for us.
Amen.


Scripture verse:

> Praise the Lord!
> Oh, give thanks to the Lord, for He is good!
> For His mercy endures forever.

> Psalm 106:1

# Life, Precious Gift!

Our life is like a shadow, a vapor, a whisper in the wind. I remember when I was but a small child. Seems just like yesterday. I look upon all my yesterdays past and I ask myself, "How can this be?" I have my past; I have the present right now. Only God knows my tomorrows, my future, and the hope of promises in my life. One day at a time I live, I breathe, I sing a new song of peace, a song of honor to the King. If not for my God I would have surely perished by now.

I am so thankful for my legs that I use to proclaim His love and salvation. I am so thankful that I have hands and arms to raise unto the heavens so high to praise Him, to honor His loving blood shed upon that old hill Calvary where victory was finally won. No more sting of death.

Every day is my time of victory, thanks to my eternal Jesus. I also thank Him for my mouth, my tongue, my words that are formed with love to declare His holy message of good news, the gospel of peace. Yes, I do indeed thank my loving Jesus for the opportunity to glory in His name until eternity past.

**Scriptures:**

I am the good shepherd. The good shepherd gives His life for the sheep.

John 10:11

I have come as a light into the world, that whoever believes in Me should not abide in darkness.

John 12:46

You call me Teacher and Lord, and you say well, for so I am.

John 13:13

# Our Life Like a Shadow

Our life like a shadow.
Our days on earth are like a shadow.
First comes the morning with the dew
as it kisses the ground with the tears from heaven
and a new day begins.
Then comes the noonday sun,
a gift from God
as the trees and flowers blossom
with the presence of God above.
Now comes the cool of the day as the ground rests in slumber
from the toil of the wind-swept day.
Finally comes the night as the moonlight shines
with beams of peace upon the midnight blue,
the deep waters of the clear blue sea.

So is our life.
Our life is like a vapor.
One moment in time, we live and then we die.
Our days are numbered.
Only God knows our birth and our death,
our beginning and our end.
Our days on earth are like a shadow.
The morning light shines forth from the sun,
the shadow appears, then comes the midnight blue,
shining forth the pale moon
upon the deep waters of the clear blue sea.
Then the clouds of glory cover the pale moon-lit skies.
As the shadow of life slowly fades away,
so are we by the grace and mercy of God
escorted by the holy angels
into the presence of God Almighty.
From life to life,
from shadow to shadow,

God is eternal in all that we are.
Our life like a shadow,
our days like a vapor,
our days like a whispering wind.
We are softly, gently, ushered into eternity
by the whirlwinds of angels' wings.
Here we humbly bow before the Holy One of God
on bended knee,
Jesus Christ, the Son of the living God.
There, for all eternity,
we will sing praises through all times
and come praising, thanking the Lamb of Glory
that we are finally home.
Yes, life like a shadow, like a whisper in the wind, like a vapor.
First we live, then we die.
It's so good to be home.
Forevermore,
until all eternity passes away
into the sea of nevermore.

**Scriptures:**

Come to Me, all you who labor and are heavy laden,
and I will give you rest. Take My yoke upon you and
learn from Me, for I am gentle and lowly in heart,
and you will find rest for your souls. For My yoke is
easy and My burden is light."

Matthew 11:28-30

# Love Is God, God Is Love!

Are you hurting today? Have you been abandoned? Going through a divorce? Do you feel like your guts are constantly being ripped out? Did you lose your mate of forty-plus years to death? Are you laying in that hospital bed listening to the doctor's report? Did the doctor say that there is no hope, you will surely die? Did you lose your little one, your innocent little child?

I say to you, God is there! He loves you! He cares for you! God says in his Word, "In the world you will have tribulation; but be of good cheer, I have overcome the world." (John 16:33b) Oh my friend, I know you are hurting, but I have the answer for you. I have the pen of a ready writer in hand for you right here upon this very moment in time. Jesus Christ is the answer. Jesus is with you! Do you not perceive it? God says in his word, "I am with you always, even to the end of the age." (Matthew 28:20b) I understand that you cannot see Him in the flesh, but you don't need to. You need to see Him in your spirit. Therein lies the answer. Therein lies your peace.

The answer of all answers is this: Do not cease to praise Him! He will help you to release the pain. He will give life and peace in place of death and pain. Jesus is real, don't listen to the world. They live only for and through the flesh. They live by the flesh. They will die in the flesh. But you, my child, my friend, you my little one, you have the answer to all of your yesterdays, all of your tomorrows. Praise Him, you are free! Praise Him, you are at peace! Praise Him, for He is yours and you are His.

**Scripture:**

27. Peace I leave with you, My peace I give to you; not as the world gives do I give to you. Let not your heart be troubled, neither let it be afraid.

John 14:27

# This Thing Called Love

What is this thing we call love?
Is it a child?
His name is Jesus.
He is Lord,
He is Savior,
He is my king,
He is my peace in the midst of the storm.
He is my refuge
in times of trouble.
He is my joy,
the very reason I live and I breathe.
He is my hope,
my God of mercy,
my God of grace.
He is my salvation.
By Him and Him alone,
His precious blood flowed
as a declaration of His eternal love and devotion to us.
He is the great and the mighty One.
The holy, the just, and the fair One.
He is the One who is worthy to be
praised,
gloried in,
honored,
respected.
The One who is worthy to be magnified,
lifted up on high forevermore.
He is Emmanuel, God is With Us.
He is our Wonderful Counselor.
He is our Mighty God.
He is our Everlasting Father.
He is the Prince of Peace.
He is the Lion of Judah.

He is the Bright and Morning Star.
What is this thing we call love?
This thing we call love is a Person,
Jesus Christ, the Son of the Living God.
The great and the mighty One.
My Lord, God, and Savior.
The great I Am.
The Alpha and Omega,
the beginning and the ending of all that is,
that was,
or ever shall be.
He is my all in all,
my creator,
my redeemer,
the very reason that I live.
I will always be Your servant, Your child, Yours to command, forevermore,
forevermore,
forevermore.

# The Way

The way I love You
is the way I need You.
The way I need You
is the way I love You.
Forever, Lord,
forever, Lord,
I will love You.
Forever, Lord,
yes, forever,
I will need You.
Who but You my King,
knows my heart,
my innermost thoughts.
Only You,
only You.
You are my peace,
my joy,
my life.
You are
my strength,
my hope,
my salvation.
If not for You,
I would perish.
If not for You,
I would surely die.
Yes, to You my Lord I say,
the way I love You
is the way I need You.
The way I need You
is the way I love You.
To know You is to love You.
To love You is to know You.

You are my King,
You are my Lord,
You are my God.
You are my God of rest,
my creator,
You are my redeemer,
You and only You
have saved me from the pit of death.
You are
my life eternal.
You are
the keeper of my heart.
You are
my next breath.
You are
the author and finisher of
my last heartbeat.
Forever and beyond,
Lord, I will love You.

**Scriptures:**

In Him also we have obtained an inheritance, being predestined according to the purpose of Him who works all things according to the counsel of His will, that we who first trusted in Christ should be to the praise of His glory.

In Him you also trusted, after you heard the word of truth, the gospel of your salvation; in whom also, having believed, you were sealed with the Holy Spirit of promise,

who is the guarantee of our inheritance until the redemption of the purchased possession, to the praise of His glory.

Ephesians 1:11-14

# My Earthly Father

Before the sands of time, God blessed me with you, Father, a man after God's own heart. You taught me of God's love and compassion throughout the ages past! Seasons come, seasons go, but I will never forget you. For you are, were, and always shall be, my father. I will always remember you as the quiet one. One word from your lips would speak volumes of the wisdom of the ages past. You, the one of peace, taught me lovingly, kindly, gently the story of Jesus Christ, the anointed One. The Son of the living God. The mighty Savior of your heart.

You were always the counselor in times of trouble. You were the protector, the provider, the one who was always there for me. You were the one who took me to church, the place of worship, praise, and love. The home and temple of the King of kings, the Lord of lords. You were the one who taught me of honesty and integrity. You taught me to always keep my promises true. I, by your example, endeavored to be on time. You taught me in my life to keep the faith. You always taught me to say that my yes is yes and my no is no. You, my loving daddy, taught me how, where, and when to fish. You said, "Son, if you drop your line down beside that big old tree stump, you'll catch your self a big one." I did as he instructed forty-two times. But who was counting? You taught me laughingly about love and marriage: "Son, just remember, what is hers is hers, and what is yours is hers. Remember this and you'll do just fine. Ha! Ha!"

Yes, my Father, Daddy, Dad, counselor and friend, this writing is for you and you alone. Good-bye, my loving father, until we meet again!

**Scriptures:**

And he said to him, "Son, you are always with me, and all that I have is yours. It was right that we should make merry and be glad, for your brother was dead and is alive again, and was lost and is found."

Luke 15:31-32

Children, obey your parents in the Lord, for this is right."Honor your father and mother," which is the first commandment with promise:"that it may be well with you and you may live long on the earth."

Ephesians 6: 1-3

So Abraham took the wood of the burnt offering and laid it on Isaac his son; and he took the fire in his hand, and a knife, and the two of them went together. But Isaac spoke to Abraham his father and said, "My father!"

And he said, "Here I am, my son."

Then he said, "Look, the fire and the wood, but where is the lamb for a burnt offering?" And Abraham said, "My son, God will provide for Himself the lamb for a burnt offering." So the two of them went together.

Genesis 22:6-8

# My Daddy

My Daddy, A man of courage,
a man of strength,
a man of love,
a man of faith untold,
a man of kindness,
a man of few words.
When spoken, his words were powerful and mighty.
His love for God and family was as deep as the oceans were blue.
His faith as high as the mountains were tall.
His dedication was as strong and constant
as the driven snow in the wintertime.
His word is and was his bond eternal and true.
His life spoke volumes in the strength and stability
of his silence.
He would speak without saying a word.
He was a silent giant.
A man of honesty and truth.
His hands were filled with the compassion of the ages past.
A silent leader of righteousness, peace, and joy.
Hands clasped together in prayer,
He taught me to love God, to honor, to respect God's holy name.
He proclaimed,
"As for me and my house, we shall now and forevermore,
Serve the Lord our God,
from here to eternity and beyond."
Now the anchor, the strength of this household
is the Lord of hosts, my loving Savior, my king, my lion of Judah.
Until the day that I shall die I say,
"I will serve, honor, and respect,
The King of glory, Jesus Christ,
The Son of the living God".

# My Father, My Daddy, My Friend

My father,
my daddy
is strong.
My father
is honest.
My father
is trustworthy.
My father
is a man of peace.
My father
is a man of encouragement.
My father
is a man of mercy.
My daddy
has hands of love.
My daddy
has hands of hope.
My daddy
has hands of strength.
My daddy's heart
is a heart for God.
My daddy's hands
guided me to church every Sunday.
My daddy's hands
lead my heart
and my life,
to receive Jesus as Lord, God. and Savior,
the great I Am,
the keeper of my heart,
the author, and finisher, of my life.

# My Mother

When I was a young man of fifteen years old, I had a motorcycle accident. I was going across a parking lot on a very cold February day with the sun glaring in my eyes. I did not know the store had blocked off an exit. I did not see the steel-reinforced cable, for the cable's coloring blended in with the pavement. I hit the cable full force. I got up on my feet by some miracle of God, rolled my motorcycle over to the nearby gas station, and told the man that I had been in an accident. The man was kind enough to call my parents. I sat down in a chair, wrenched in pain. My parents picked me up and carried me to the truck. All I told them was, "Take me home, and I will be fine."

My mother and my father knew better. They raced to the hospital emergency room. Immediately the nurses and doctors started working on me. The conclusions of the damage were internal lacerations of the spleen, liver, pancreas, kidneys, and so on--you get the picture. I should have died. By the grace and mercy of a mother's prayers, I lived.

A couple of days later while I was in the hospital, Richard, a good friend of mine, hit the same cable. Four hours later, he died on the operating table. I did not understand. Why did I live and he died? God had his reasons. Ours is to only call out unto the heavens to God Almighty and wonder, why, God, why? The conclusion was that I lived and others died. There were a reported seventeen accidents on that very spot where I crashed. After my friend died, the store decided to take down the cable.

The reason I have shared this brief moment of my private history is because I wanted to point out to you that in sunshine and in shadow, in the good times, and in the bad, God is there. We may not always understand why things happen, but this much I do know, my friend Richard is alive and well. He does now live and breathe before the feet of Jesus Christ, his loving, caring, Lord, God, and Savior. Richard is now more alive than I could ever imagine being here on this earth, our temporary home.

God is here right now upon this very moment in time. Do not cry, do not weep. Jesus has conquered the grave, the sting of death.

I comfort you, I proclaim, whoever you may be, whoever this writing is for, do not cry! Do not weep! Rejoice! For as Jesus has been raised from the dead by the Holy Spirit, so has your little one, friend, husband, wife, whoever it may be, and is waiting at heaven's door with the anointing presence of Jesus your hope, your peace, your joy!

For approximately ninety-nine days my dearest mother comforted me, wiped my fevered brow, kissed my hand, loved me openly and tenderly with all that was within her. My mother sheltered me from the storms of life in those days. She nursed me back to health by the anointed prayers of a mother's love and devotion.

My mother raised, gave, dedicated me up to God, and God, by His mercy and His grace, gave me back to my mother!

**Scriptures:**

But Hannah did not go up, for she said to her husband, "Not until the child is weaned; then I will take him, that he may appear before the Lord and remain there forever."

1 Samuel 1:22

Call to Me, and I will answer you, and show you great and mighty things, which you do not know.

Jeremiah 33:3

To everything there is a season,
A time for every purpose under heaven:

Ecclesiastes 3:1

# My Mother

My mother,
Mom.
My mother,
love.
My mother,
protector.
My mother,
gentle.
My mother,
kind.
My mother,
the touch.
My mother,
her hands.
My mother,
my mom.
My mother,
she loved me with kisses from heaven.
My mother,
she protected me,
shielded me from the storms of life.
My mother,
she was gentle.
If I would skin my knee,
she would kiss the pain away.
My mother
was kind.
She was always there to share a loving word
of hope and peace.
My mother
had the touch of Jesus,
anointed unto the sands of time and beyond all eternity.
My mother,

the hands of peace,
the hands of joy,
the hands of love,
the hands of caring bliss.
My mother,
my mom.
The one who loved me tender.
The protector of my heart and life.
The gentle one.
The kind one.
The touch and feeling of which
only a mother's hands could fulfill
from here to eternity past.
Amen!

# Ninety-Nine Days

Ninety-nine days, my mother. she did pray.
She was always there for me!
Ninety-nine days, death was at my door.
She was always there for me!
Ninety-nine days, she cried out to God.
She was always there for me!
Ninety-nine days. my mother spoke the Word.
She was always there for me!
Ninety-nine days, the battle surged
with the pain of the ages past.
The story goes on.
My mother and my holy Jesus versus death.
She was always there for me!
Ninety-nine days, I was on her mind.
She was always there for me!
Ninety-nine days, God was there,
hearing a mother's heaven-sent prayers.
She was always there for me!
Ninety-nine days, the angels sang.
Ninety-nine days, my mother did
sing, glorify, honor, the Lord her God.
Yes, indeed, ninety-nine days, my mother did
praise Jesus's holy name.
Ninety-nine days,the Lord heard her prayers,
heard her cry,
heard His Word proclaimed from upon high.
From her very lips
she spoke life through the Holy Spirit,
through Jesus.
She proclaimed,
"My son shall live and not die.
He will,
he shall,

proclaim the Word of God from this moment on
until earth and sky,
cloud and rain,
the sun above and all within and without
perish into all eternity and beyond!"

Yes, oh God,
my mother, heaven sent by your holy decree
was always there for me!

# My God Lives and Breathes Forever!

I testify to you today, upon this next breath which my loving God has created, that my Jesus, my king, my source, my supply, lives and He breathes. He is the testimony of my household. Let the world cheat, lie, die in their sins. As for me and my house, we will love, honor, praise, adore, and cherish, the name of Jesus Christ, for He is the reason I live. I do not live for money, for it will fade away and burn with the tides of time eternal. I do not live for the world and stuff, for it is built to perish throughout the ages. But as for me and my family, through His precious blood, we shall live within and without forever by the hand of God Almighty, my peace, my eternal life. I do glorify my king. Because of Him and Him alone do we live and breathe because of the eternal sacrifice, the lamb for the slaughter. Jesus is the Rose of Sharon, the Light of the World, the one of hope until all eternity shall pass away, which will be nevermore. Amen!

**Scriptures:**

And if it seems evil to you to serve the Lord, choose for yourselves this day whom you will serve, whether the gods which your fathers served that were on the other side of the River, or the gods of the Amorites, in whose land you dwell. But as for me and my house we will serve the Lord.

Joshua 24:15

Lift up your eyes to the heavens, And look on the earth beneath. For the heavens will vanish away like smoke. The earth will grow old like a garment, And those who dwell in it will die in like manner, But my salvation will be forever, And My righteousness will not be abolished.

Isaiah 51:6

I keep Your precepts and Your testimonies, For all my ways are before You.

Psalm 119: 168

# God the Essence of My Life

The wind blows,
as the restless leaves take flight into the heavens above,
only to be met by the coolness of the autumn breeze of glory.
As the morning dew caresses the green grass,
the sun rises high in the sky
with the warmth and beauty of the Creator Elohim,
the great and the mighty One.
The keeper of all that is, shall be, or ever was.
There are those who tell me that God is alive.
There are those who tell me that God is dead.
People tell me he is like the watchmaker,
with His mighty skills of creation,
who has made his creation only to be observed,
never to help the weary, the helpless, the destitute.
People tell me that his miracles, his healing hands,
have been silenced by the passing of the ages,
that he has decided to simply ignore the cries of His children.
I, for one, am a child of the most high living, caring God.
He is always mindful of me,
the great and mighty One,
the holy,
the just,
the fair One.
As for me and my house we will proclaim
that Jesus Christ, the Son of the living God, is alive and well.
He is our king,
our source,
our supply,
our abundance.
If you are going to try to talk me out of believing
in my Lord, God, and Savior, you're too late.
If you want me to believe He does not heal today,
you're wrong.

I am healed by the blood of the Lamb
and by the word of my testimony!
My God,
My king,
is Alpha and Omega,
He knows my beginning, and He has ordained my end.
For me to die is only my beginning, my gain.
I will live throughout all eternity with my loving Jesus,
my Savior, my Lord, my God, my friend.
He does not only observe me, He loves me.
I will always believe that my king is there for me.
He has spoken to me several times in my life
saying in His holy Word,
"Call upon Me in the day of trouble; I will deliver you,
and you shall glorify Me."
I will always trust, always believe, that You are the great I Am
The keeper of my life,
my heart,
my peace,
for today and throughout all eternity.

### Scriptures:

So Jesus said to them again, "Peace to you! As the Father has sent Me, I also send you."

And when He said this, He breathed on them, and said, "Receive the Holy Spirit."

John 20:21-22

"Call upon Me in the day of trouble; I will deliver you, and you shall glorify Me."

Psalms 50:15

# My Loving Holy Spirit

Holy, Holy, Holy Spirit, my Friend from ages past, You have come to love me with Your very presence. You have come to answer me when I ask the question, "Why God, why?" You are eternal, the part of the Godhead, the Holy Trinity that is with me day in and day out.

When I am sad and looking for joy, you open up the scriptures as I look up to the heavens above, the valleys below, an, because of your precious love for me, I praise, I honor, I adore my God of Glory. Who am I, oh Holy, Holy, Holy Spirit, to have the right to call out to You for help in times of desperation?

Again, my Counselor, my friend, my joy, my peace, guides me gently, lovingly, softly, with all compassion to the scriptures to show me the answers that I need in this world of confusion and turmoil. The Holy Spirit is the One Who raised Jesus from the grave. The Holy Spirit is the One who leads me oh so gently to meet Jesus Christ my Savior, the Light of the World, the keeper of my heart, the one whose blood kissed the ground so passionately to save me from death, hell, and the grave to give me peace like a river. He broke the dam, which harnessed the waters of eternal life. By Jesus's blood, by His bodily sacrifice, I am free, I am whole, I am complete!

I thank you Holy, Holy, Holy Spirit for introducing me to my King Jesus. If not for you, I would have passed into all eternity, lost and forgotten, in a land of destruction forever. Loving Holy Spirit, you are indeed my very present friend in time of danger!

**Scriptures:**

However, when He, the Spirit of truth has come, He will guide you into all truth; for he will not speak on his own authority, but whatever He hears He will speak; and He will tell you things to come. He will glorify Me, for He will take of what is Mine and declare it to you.

John 16:13,14

# Holy Spirit

Who are you, Holy Spirit, but my Teacher,
The One who proclaims the Word of God to my spirit
softly and gently in a way that I will understand?
Who are you but my counselor
when I cry out in the midst of my confusion,
holding,
sharing,
caring,
giving me the answers that I need
in my hour of desperation and weakness,
for You are my all and all.
You hold the secrets of the universe within Your very hands.
You are the God of passion,
always ready to edify,
always ready to lift me up,
always ready to shower me through all eternity
with your compassionate, un-abounding love.
You are the One who anoints me with Your oil of
gladness,
peace,
and joy.
You are the God with unlimited power to rescue me,
to hold me close in times of danger.
I thank you,
I love you,
I need you Holy Spirit!

# My New Life

There was a time in my life that I hurt so bad I thought I was going to die. Have you ever felt like that? There was a time when I was so wrenched with pain and anguish, my insides actually felt like they were being pulled out. I was so distraught I could hardly breathe. I had run away from God for such a long time from lack of knowledge, not knowing the true, true, loving God. The God I knew back then was a threatening God. One false move and He would send down his whip of thunder and destroy you. He was the kind of God you loved because you were afraid of Him. The kind of God that, if you were bad, would send you to hell or put cancer on you to teach you a lesson. Is that the kind of God you serve?

Let's stop right there for a moment. The teaching I had been taught was wrong. You might think, "You mean you would actually say that men of God would actually teach such things?" Yes, we have been deceived. There are men of God that mean well, but they were taught incorrectly. Think for a moment: Why would a loving, caring God send His only Son to show you what true love is, even to the point of his own Son's death to save you from your sins, and then turn around and smite you with a mighty blow to hurt you? Did Jesus not say in His word, "If you have seen Me, then you have seen the Father?" Jesus went about this earth healing, loving, and caring. Jesus here on earth was a God of love and compassion. Time after time, Jesus had a listening ear to every need of the people. Think about how God is. He does not grade on a curve. That is man's way. God's way is not conditional. He does not love you by your performance. He loves you, period. He loves you just the way you are. He made you to be who you are. Stop running toward religion and run to God. If you have run away from home, then simply come back to Him, tell him you're sorry, and start over again. He will not scold you, beat you, and knock you senseless. He will simply love you and say "Welcome back into the arms of My love and compassion forevermore even unto eternity."

If you have never been saved before, it's easy: simply believe in who He is, thank Him for His blood that was shed for your sins, surrender your life, your heart and all that you are over to him right now - not later - right now. Now is the day of your new beginning, your salvation. Why would you want to wait for such a beautiful gift of God's eternal love - eternal life with him forever? You may say, "But you don't know what I have done!" You're right, I don't know, but God knows. He will not dump you because of your sin. He came specifically to die for *you*, for *you* personally! Don't you see that? Surrender, He is there for you. Surrender, He is Lord! Surrender, He is God. Surrender, He is love. Surrender, He is the answer to all problems, all of your yesterdays. He is the answer to all of your tomorrows. Jesus was the Lamb for the slaughter for you. He is, was, and forever shall be your answer. Surrender!

Jesus, my sweet Jesus, my king, my source, my supply, and my abundance, the love of my life, He saved me, He comforted me, He made me brand-new, and I have never been the same since. I was sitting on my bed hurting, crying, and dying inside. I knew God had been trying to get me to come back to Him, but the answer was always the same: "Not now," or "I'm not ready." I was afraid of God. What would He do to me if I did come back to Him? Isn't that a crazy way of thinking? I was away from God in sin, and I was concerned about what He would do to me if I came back to Him.

On that final day of hurt, pain, and despair, all I said was, "Okay, Lord." He knew that meant I was coming back to Him. When I said that, I had an experience with God that I had never experienced before in my whole entire life. God's love, God's presence, His very being, entered the room. It was simply a knowing that I knew this was God, this was love, this was Who the true living God truly was. My God's holy presence covered me, first over my hair as it tingled from the warmth and presence of His being. Then, as He continued down to cover my ears, all sounds were muffled. Then He slowly and lovingly covered the rest of my body. This was truly the God I never knew. This was truly the God of whom I was never taught. This was my true, true, loving, caring, compassionate God. Oh, my friends, if I could only express the love that I felt in the room that day! Words cannot express what I experienced that day.

Scientists try every day to prove there is no God. My friends, I proclaim that Jesus Christ the Son of the living God is alive, He lives,

He breathes, He is the keeper of all that I am and all that I shall ever be. He is alive. He lives within my heart. Don't listen to the scoffers who proclaim man is god. Don't listen to the scientists who proclaim God doesn't exist or that all gods are the same. Don't listen to men who proclaim that God is only nature and we are all gods. Believe in the true, loving, caring God who died for you and me on the cross. The One who, by His blood, His bodily sacrifice, His mercy, His grace, by His eternal love for you, saved you from death, hell, and the grave. Yes, my little ones, it's time for a new beginning! Believe in the true and living God who loved you unto His very last breath, then was raised from the dead to live again forevermore by the power of the Holy Spirit to complete the final process for your eternal salvation. Yes, your new beginning is finally knowing the real God. The God of love, mercy, and grace. Jesus Christ, the Anointed One. The Son of the Living God.

**Scriptures:**

Enter into His gates with thanksgiving,
And into His courts with praise.
Be thankful to Him, and bless His name.

For the Lord is good;
His mercy is everlasting,
And His truth endures to all generations.

Psalm 100:4,5

Then Jesus cried out and said, "He who believes in Me, believes not in Me but in Him who sent Me. And he who sees Me sees Him who sent Me. I have come as a light into the world, that whoever believes in Me should not abide in darkness.

John 12:44-46

Let not your heart be troubled; you believe in God, believe also in Me.

John 14:1

Thomas said to Him, "Lord, we do not know where You are going, and how can we know the way?"

Jesus said to him, "I am the way, the truth, and the life. No one comes to the Father except through Me.

"If you had known Me, you would have known My Father also; and from now on you know Him and have seen Him."

Philip said to Him, "Lord, show us the Father, and it is sufficient for us."

Jesus said to him, "Have I been with you so long, and yet you have not known Me, Philip? He who has seen Me has seen the Father; so how can you say, 'Show us the Father'? Do you not believe that I am in the Father, and the Father in Me? The words that I speak to you I do not speak on My own authority; but the Father who dwells in Me does the works. Believe Me that I am in the Father and the Father in Me, or else believe Me for the sake of the works themselves.

John 14:5-11

Abide in Me, and I in you. As the branch cannot bear fruit of itself, unless it abides in the vine, neither can you, unless you abide in Me.

I am the vine, you are the branches. He who abides in Me, and I in him, bears much fruit; for without Me you can do nothing.

John 15:4,5

"As the Father loved Me, I also have loved you; abide in My love.

John 15:9

To You I will cry, O Lord my Rock:
Do not be silent to me,
Lest, if You are silent to me,
I become like those who go down to the pit.

Psalm 28:1

Give unto the Lord, O you mighty ones,
Give unto the Lord glory and strength.
Give unto the Lord the glory due to His name;
Worship the Lord in the beauty of holiness.

Psalm 29:1-2

I will extol You, O Lord, for You have lifted me up,
And have not let my foes rejoice over me.
O Lord my God, I cried out to You,
And You healed me.
O Lord, You brought my soul up from the grave;
You have kept me alive, that I should not go down
to the pit.
Sing praise to the Lord, you saints of His,
And give thanks at the remembrance of His holy
name.

Psalm 30:1-4

My heart is overflowing with a good theme;
I recite my composition concerning the King;
My tongue is the pen of a ready writer.

Psalm 45:1

Hear my cry, O God;
Attend to my prayer.
From the end of the earth I will cry to You,
When my heart is overwhelmed;
Lead me to the rock that is higher than I.

Psalm 61:1-2

I will praise You, O Lord, with my whole heart;
I will tell of all Your marvelous works.

Psalm 9:1

# Today

Today is my new beginning.
I look to my new life for patience, love, and security,
for my beloved ones.
I try to live life as it comes,
to listen to the bird of peace,
to heed its call of danger.
I look to my right, I see only fear.
I look to my left, I see hatred.
What should I do, what can I say?
I look above to the heavens for guidance.
I seek Your way, Your will and Your plan.
I praise Your name.
I worship with the voice of the angels.
I praise,
I worship,
I surrender to Your calling,
for You and You alone are the way, the truth, and the life.
Yes, out of the depths of my very being, I surrender
my heart,
my soul,
my spirit,
my very existence.
You are indeed Lord God Almighty,
the Holy One,
the righteous One,
Alpha and Omega,
the beginning and the end of my life eternal.
I surrender to Your will, oh God.
For who holds my last breath in His hands but You.
I am yours,
I am yours,
I am yours,
forevermore,
Amen!

# My Wife

My wife, the one whom I have loved for some thirty-plus years, is not only my loving bride, she has also been my best friend. Through sunshine and shadow, thick and thin, good times and bad, we have always been there for each other. God is the head of our household. When we have problems, as do all marriages, we call out to Him in prayer. He is the one who sets sail away from the furious winds to steer us clear of trouble, to find the answers for life's storms. I praise God every day for His loving-kindness. He has given me a helpmate who enjoys life to its fullest. She includes me in every event in life (except shopping, if you know what I mean).

We both know that either my wife or myself will go first to heaven to be with the Lord. You will notice in this section that I have written on times when one or the other of us has gone away to be with our loving Savior, Jesus the King.

The reason I have developed these writings from my heart is because I remember my dad, who is so strong, who never cried, bursting into tears over the passing of my dearest mother. My mother was not only a loving Christian, she was also my dad's best friend.

You see, when our loved ones die, the grief is truly heart-breaking. I write to comfort you and to give peace to the brokenhearted in time of need. This is the time you need to know that Jesus truly loves you through all of your pain and hardship.

**Scriptures:**

whereas you do not know what will happen tomorrow. For what is your life? It is even a vapor that appears for a little time and then vanishes away.

James 4:14

Who can find a virtuous wife?
For her worth is far above rubies.

Proverbs 31:10

# Hello, Good-bye

Hello, good-bye, my love.
Seems just like yesterday since we met.

Hello, good-bye, my love.
First we were young of years, young of heart,
and now we are of the golden years of peace, harmony,
and surrender to the years to come.
We were once full of life,
and now the energetic tendencies of our youth
are gone away like a whisper in the wind.
I have loved you, my dearest little one,
crown of my peace.
I have cared for you from without and from within
my innermost being.
You are the joy of my life,
The red, red rose of beauty and grace.
You and only you
were the chosen one,
the kind one,
the loving one.
You were the gentle breeze in the morning,
the precious dew in all its glory
that kisses the ground with all love, and compassion,
care and devotion.
You are now, and ever shall be, my gift from God.
Now my love, and even now
you have gone away,
like a mist with the tides of time eternal
into the loving precious arms of Jesus Christ,
the Son of the living God,
Our Lord,
Our King,
Our Peace.

Hello, good-by, my love.

In the distant reaches of my tomorrows, I will find you again, and we will say hello, with no more good-byes,

holding fast to our Lord and his promises,

from here to eternity, and beyond!

Amen!

Amen!

and Amen!

# Thank You for My Wife

Today I sing a song of laughter.
Tomorrow brings me a song of love, truth,
and solemn pleasures.
I look to the sky for the bird of peace.
I seek not harm but victory upon the happiness
of two in such a deep love for each other.
I pray for life in its fullest essence
as the warming sunshine,
as the truth and prosperity of men through the ages.
May the warmth of the sunshine
upon you and your beauty
show forth a path of glory
which you have chosen to follow.
May your path be filled with warmth and happiness
from here to eternity past.

Thank you, Lord, for the one You have chosen for me.
This creation you have called woman
has brought me love, joy, peace,
life to its fullest potential.
Thank you Lord, I am grateful.
I am honored.
I'm amazed,
I'm astonished
that you would personally gift me
with your fondest possession,
my wife.
I do indeed, humbly, and respectfully
thank you forevermore,
my dearest Lord God and Savior.
Jesus my Light, my peace, my hope, my everything.
I will thank You, praise You, and lift up
Your holy precious name
from here throughout the ages to come and beyond.
Amen!

# The Letter

To my dearest darling:
This letter is dedicated to you,
my best friend,
my wife,
the love of my life.
I have some things to share with you,
from this old heart of mine.
When we first met, we were young of heart, full of life.
Now I am old, filled with memories of yesterdays past.
Thoughts of joy,
thoughts of my best friend.
My, oh my, the fun we have shared with each other.
Thank you, God, for all the pleasant memories of yesteryear.
I have tried my best to be a husband of all husbands to you
in the mornings of your life when the dove sang
its song of peace and joy.
In the evenings of your life I have tried to be
your knight in shining armor,
shielding you from the cruelty of the world
and all its problems.
I have done my very best to be yours and only yours.
And I am confident in saying that I believe and I know
that you loved me with all of your heart as well.
Jesus is, has been, and always will be
the anchor to hold us steady in the storms of life.
I thank God we have always been loyal to our children as well.
A beautiful daughter, a handsome young man,
our children have always been beautiful in our sight,
and in the sight of the Lord our God, our King.
I intend to thank God daily for the gift of life.
The gift of holding each other close through all these years.
My darling,
my friend,

my love,
my life,
this letter I'm writing to you now may not make it to you.
I do love you and miss you very much.
I suppose I will have to deliver it my self to you,
special delivery,
heaven-sent, the love of my life, my gift from God
How right it is to care.
How sweet it is to have memories of togetherness.
The love of my life, my gift from God!

# The Love of My Life

How right it is to care.
How sweet it is to have memories of togetherness.
How distant yesterday seems.
How beautiful it is to see the sunrise in the morning with you.
Rainy nights,
cold winter days,
and hot summer days -
they come and they go.
But remember our God, our King,
our joy,
our peace,
the love of our life,
for He is the One who keeps us dry
from the rainy days of sorrow.
He is the warmth of the blanket on the cold, dreary winter days.
He is the One who removes the sweat from our brow.
He is the One who walks with us in the cool of the morning,
speaking to us with His gentle whisper of peace.
Yes, we glorify Your holy name,
for You are the keeper of our marriage, all that is good.
You are the One Who is ever-present.
Always loving,
always caring,
always blessing,
Amen.

# My Wife

Hand in hand
I will walk with you.
I will talk with you
as I bestow my love to you.
I will shelter you from the storms of time.
I will be with you.
I will care for you.
I will be with you through eternity past.
I will be yours and you will be mine.
I will be your shield.
I will be your refuge in times of trouble.
I decree, I speak upon this moment in time,
even if I should perish,
fade away into the glorious riches of God's eternity,
I will search for you.
I will find you,
for you are my wife.
From here to eternity,
forevermore,
forevermore,
forevermore!

# My Wife, Gift of God Eternal

My wife, gift of God eternal,
second only to God above.
I thank You, my Lord God and Savior
for my loving, caring, bride of thirty years plus.
I thank you for her smile
that summons the joy and beauty of all creation,
to cry out
in peace,
love,
and serenity.
I thank you for her being,
the breath of life,
a touch of the Master Potter's hands.
For with her eyes
and hair so fair,
she commands the dew from the heavens so blue,
the rains from the east,
to draw near to the west, just to be near her.
She is my bride,
my only bride,
the joy of my heart, life, and soul.
And I will shower her with all my love,
as it flows like a river,
overflowing the banks of eternity past.

Yes, my love,
this poem is for you and you alone.
For you are my true love, my wife,
gift from God Eternal.
Forevermore,
forevermore,
forevermore,
until I here the calling

and the leading of my Master's hand,
leading me on into tomorrow's kingdom of peace and rest.
So humbly and respectfully,
my dearest Lord Jesus Christ,
the Son of the Living God,
I do thank you.
I do prayerfully thank you,
for my wife eternal,
the gift from God,
creation from the Potter's wheel of His loving-kindness.

# With Each Rising Sun

With each rising sun
there is a new dawn,
A new morning, a new day.
A time when the dew kisses the ground
with the tears from heaven above.

With each rising sun
there is a new dawn,
a new morning, a new day.
Another day to see the sunrise.
The colors of glory
upon the tapestry of the sky, the tapestry of God.

With each rising sun
there is a new dawn,
a new morning, a new day.
Another opportunity to hold you close, my darling,
to tell you how much I care.

Yes, with each rising sun
there is a new dawn arisin',
a new morning, a new day
to tell you I love you,
to tell you I care,
to tell you I need you,
to tell you I am yours,
forevermore until time passes away.

Yes, my love, there is a new morn a-comin',
a new day,
a great and mighty day of the Lord on the horizon.
Yes, my wife,
my friend,

my love,
bone of my bone,
flesh of my flesh.
I am yours and you are mine.
I love you, and you love me.
To each other we are a gift from God.
I thank you, my Lord God and Savior,
my loving king, for your handiwork.
I am so thankful for you, my love,
for you are truly the gift from heaven above,
that was created for me alone.
Forevermore, I will glory in the name of the Lord my God
who has seen fit to bless me with
my wife,
my friend,
my love!

# Man Calls Out to God

Are you sad today? God is there for you. Are you crying tears of loss today? Jesus is your joy. Are the walls of this world crashing in on you? The Holy Spirit is your comforter, your peace in the midst of the storm. Have you lost a loved one? Have you lost your home to the world system? Have you lost your job because the boss was unfair, immoral, and didn't like you because you were a Christian? Rejoice, God is there!

You say, "I can't see Him. I need to see Him physically right now. I need to hold Him, touch His hand, behold His face. " He is there for you whether you see Him or not. He lives within your heart.

You say to me, "The bills are piling up, I need for God to help me, to talk to me, to be there for me." He is there. Don't go by what you see or what you feel. Go by the eternal things of God, His Word. Is it so surprising that you have problems? Remember what Jesus said in his Word? Jesus said that in this world you would have trouble, but to be of good cheer, for He has overcome the world. Yes, you will have trouble in this world. Don't blame God. You are in a system controlled by Satan himself.

You may ask me, "How do you know"? Because I have been there before, right where you are. Your answer is prayer, praise, and the Word of God. In all things, give thanks to the Lord your God. Praise Him. He will see you through. Storms don't last forever. With God's help, He will pick you up, dust you off, dry your tears, and anoint you with the oil of gladness. What I am trying to tell you is that in the tough times of life - and we will have tough times - it seems like He doesn't care. We are always trying to do things our own way to solve our own problems. Allow God to heal the hurt and the wounds that the world sometimes sends your way.

**Scriptures:**

"Therefore I say to you, do not worry about your life, what you will eat or what you will drink; nor about your body, what you will put on. Is not life more than food and the body more than clothing? Look at the birds of the air, for they neither sow nor reap nor gather into barns; yet your heavenly Father feeds them. Are you not of more value than they? Which of you by worrying can add one cubit to his stature?

"So why do you worry about clothing? Consider the lilies of the field, how they grow: they neither toil nor spin; and yet I say to you that even Solomon in all his glory was not arrayed like one of these. Now if God so clothes the grass of the field, which today is, and tomorrow is thrown into the oven, will He not much more clothe you, O you of little faith?

"Therefore do not worry, saying, 'What shall we eat?' or 'What shall we drink?' or 'What shall we wear?' For after all these things the Gentiles seek. For your heavenly Father knows that you need all these things. But seek first the kingdom of God and His righteousness, and all these things shall be added to you. Therefore do not worry about tomorrow, for tomorrow will worry about its own things. Sufficient for the day is its own trouble."

Matthew 6:25-34

"Do not fear, little flock, for it is your Father's good pleasure to give you the kingdom. Sell what you have and give alms; provide yourselves money bags which do not grow old, a treasure in the heavens that does not fail, where no thief approaches nor moth destroys. For where your treasure is, there your heart will be also."

Luke 12:32-34

# My Refuge, My Hope

God of mercy,
God of grace,
God of love, gentleness, and kindness,
God of peace, joy,
God of patience
and long-suffering,
Creator of all things both above and below.
You are the keeper of my heart,
my refuge, in times of trouble.
The One who rescues me
from the castle dark, the dungeon of death.
It is You I place my hope in.
You, and you alone, do I trust.
I ask of You, my loving, caring Lord God and Savior,
rescue me from the enemy's schemes
and his plans of destruction for my life.
Do not allow him to take
the very breath that you have blessed me with.
Please Lord, rescue me.
Release my mind from the chains that hold me captive.
Remove the bands and shackles that torture and torment me.
There is no hope,
no peace,
no life,
no rescue
without Your mighty hand of righteousness
to uphold, protect and save me.
I cry out to you like a lamb for the slaughter.
Rescue me!
Save me!
My enemies, they glee and they smile with evil pleasure
in their evil plans to surround and destroy me.
Though the evil ones of this wicked land may slay me,
I will trust in salvation from their wicked hands of war.
For you are my God, my protector, my hope in times of trouble!

# Restore Me, Oh God

Restore me, oh God!
Restore this broken body.
Restore this sorrowed heart.
Restore my life, my being, my existence.
Restore me and all that I am,
for I am wounded, hurt, torn asunder.
Restore me, oh God
from the cares, the distractions,
the corruption of this old sin-ridden world.
If not you, oh God, who will rescue me?
If not you, oh God, who will restore me?
If not you, oh God, who will refresh this
torn, tattered, desolate body of mine?
If not you, oh God,
who will heal, replenish, and renew
this sorrowed, angered, tortured heart of mine?
If not you, oh God,
who will give life, hope, and peace
to this ravaged soul, this distressed life of mine?
Only you!
Only you!
Only you can heal the broken-hearted,
set the captives free,
give life where there is death!
You, oh God, and only You, are my refuge.
You, oh God, and only You, are my fortress.
You, oh God, and only You, are my shield.
Yes, you are Lord God and Savior,
my help in a very present time of danger.
I will follow,
I will honor,
I will surrender to Your calling,
from here to eternity past.
Amen!

# The Master Stone Cutter

The Master Stone Cutter,
the Cornerstone of my life,
the Keeper of my spirit, soul, and body,
the Architect of my life,
the keeper of all that I am.
The Master Stone Cutter
chips away with all diligence.
The Master Stone Cutter
chips away with precision.
The Master Stone Cutter
sculpts and creates with all kindness,
with His gentle hands of love and compassion.
The Master Stone Cutter
with the wisdom of the ages
gently cuts and trims
the troubled areas of my life
to bring me peace in the midst of the storm.
The hands of the Master Creator
turns my heart of stone into a heart of clay.
He molds, shapes, cuts and trims
the heart of my soul
to rescue, to protect,
to keep me from the perilous journey
into all of my tomorrows.
He is gentle.
He is kind.
He is loving.
He is caring.
I am His, and He is mine.
I was bought by a price,
by the precious blood of the King.
Jesus Christ,
The Master Stone Cutter,

The sculptor,
The architect,
The cornerstone,
The author of my life eternal.
I have surrendered all that I am to You,
for you are faithful and just.
He who has begun a good work in me
will carry it on to completion
until the day of His coming.
Forever I will praise Him.
Forever I will worship Him.
Forever I shall lift Him up,
until the eve of eternity has passed away.

# The Symbol

The symbol
of life divine.
The symbol
of life eternal.
The symbol
of peace everlasting.
The symbol
of salvation.
The symbol
of hope forevermore -
the cross, the tree,
the place of sin my master, my Savior, bore for me.
The cross, the tree,
the place of torment and pain,
meant for me.
He did pay.
The cross, the tree,
the place of love, and sacrifice, peace and brokenness.
The symbol
of life divine, life eternal, peace everlasting,
salvation eternal, is mine for now, and for all times
because of the blood of Jesus Christ the eternal One,
the loving One,
the caring One, my redeemer true.
The cross, the tree,
the place where my Master paid the price
for all of my sins.
The place of His torment, pain, sacrifice, and brokenness,
has made it possible to have His
love,
peace,
eternal glory
for now and throughout all eternity.

I am thankful, my Lord, for Your loving-kindness,
Your mercy,
Your grace,
Your gentleness.
The things of which I cannot ever repay.
You, oh Lord,
You are my king,
my Savior,
my redeemer.
Please, my loving Jesus,
please, never let go of my hand!

# Vindicate Me Oh Lord

Vindicate me, oh Lord my God
from the hands of my enemy.
Vindicate me, oh Lord my God
from the chains of this world.
Rescue me, oh my Lord God and Savior
from the tongue, the snare of all my oppressors.
Rescue me from this castle dark,
this rock of torment.
Free me from the dust of death.
The prison of Sheol – it calls out to me in my darkest hour.
Comfort me, oh Lord God creator,
redeemer of my soul,
with Your oil of gladness,
for my time is short,
the enemy is near,
even at the door.
He closes in like the hunter,
his prey to destroy,
and even to devour my very life.
Yes, vindicate me, oh Lord God of my salvation.
I will trust in Your holy name.
I will praise You,
I will worship You, yes,
and I will honor You.
I will wait upon the Lord my God my strength.
Yes, I will take up the cup of salvation,
I will call upon the name of the Lord,
my peace,
my joy,
my hope,
my present help in a desperate time of trouble.
I do believe, and I do speak, that
you are Lord,

you are God,
You are Savior,
by Your blood,
by Your name,
by Your word.
For you are the keeper of
my heart,
my mind,
my body,
my soul,
and my spirit.
Yes, you are
my champion,
my help in a very present time of trouble and danger.
Yes, I will trust You.
Yes, I will praise You.
Yes, I will worship You,
For You are my God.

# My Very Present Help

Oh dearest God, how many times have You rescued me? You and only You have been my help in times of crisis.

I was in the electronics business for twenty-five years. It was nothing to be laid off. When work was plentiful, I would work overtime constantly. When work was playing out, I would be laid off. Then the times of trouble would come upon us. Sure, the companies would call me back, but it would be six months to a year later. The only people that truly understand the pressure that I am speaking of are people that have been laid off before. Believe me, when you have no money coming in, it's very tough. God would sustain me by getting little two-day jobs here and there until I was able to find something permanent.

But I thank my God, he was always there to provide for me and my family one day at a time. One day, we even got our water cut off with no money whatsoever to pay the bill. Our choice was to buy food or do without the water. We chose buying food. Then I received a check in the mail from a mighty man of God. He wrote a note that stated "Michael, God told me to give you one hundred fifty dollars to see you through your tough times." I had not seen this gentleman for four years. Praise God, He is so good to us in times of trouble. Another great lady of God did not know of our crisis either. Would you like to know what happened? She presented us with a one-hundred-dollar Walmart card. By the way, we were still tithing off of what we had. We would tithe our time since we had no money to speak of.

Well, because of God's intervention through other people, things got better. I'm pleased to report that I have been working steadily for twelve years now with no layoffs.

Scripture:

And my God shall supply all your need according to His riches in glory by Christ Jesus.

Philippians 4:19

# In Sunshine and in Shadow

In sunshine and in shadow,
by the pale moon's light,
in daytime and night.
From the sunshine morn,
to the noonday heat,
to the cool of the evening hour.
I journeyed long,
I journeyed hard,
throughout this sin-ridden world.
I've been high atop the rocky mountains blue,
I've been low, down in the valley so green.
I've been happy,
I've been sad.
Through it all, I've had the Lord to be
my shield,
my refuge,
my strength,
my rampart,
my shadow of comfort in the midday sunshine
hot and blistering bold.
I have a song in my heart,
a jump and a twist in my step,
as I go through this old world.
For He lives in me.
Jesus touches my heart and my life with the
oil of gladness,
the anointing of joy,
His presence of peace.

In sunshine and in shadow,
In daytime and night,
by the sunshine in daytime,

and the moon-lit skies by night,
in the sunshine morn to the noon-day heat
to the cool of the evening hour of the midnight blue.
I journeyed long,
I journeyed hard,
over the mountains of the moon,
and down the valley of the shadow.
There do I now rest forevermore with
the King,
the Savior,
the Creator,
of the rocky mountains so high,
the valleys of green so low.
With You now my keeper of my
spirit,
my soul,
my heart.
Forevermore unto the eternal rising of the sunshine
and shadow of all eternity beyond.

# Lord, I Have Come to Be Yours

Lord, I have come
to speak to You,
to be with You,
to walk with You in the cool of the day.

Lord, I have come
to praise You,
to love You,
to worship You.

Lord, I have come
to remember You,
to thank You,
for Your protection,
Your mercy,
Your grace,
In the midst of the storms of my life.

Lord, I have come
to trust You,
obey You,
and to follow You.

Yes, my Lord,
my God,
my Savior,
I have come to be with You,
for You are my all in all in my life
as I go forth from day to day
through this journey we call life.

Yes, my Lord,
I have come to talk to You,
fellowship with You,
praise You,
worship You,
love You,
remember You,
trust You,
obey You,
follow You,
for You are the answer to all my todays
and the strength for all my tomorrows.
You are the great I am of all eternity.
My ever-present God.

# Where Were You, God?

Whenever you are down and out and you don't believe God anymore, this is what He would say to you:

"I have always been there for you. The world has crushed in on you like a flood. I saved you. Do you not perceive the countless number of times I have hid you in the cleft of the rock eternal? Have you not seen My mighty hand of gentleness, compassion, and love towards you? Lift up your eyes to the heavens. I am, I was, and forever shall be with you. I am always there for you. I send my angels to watch over you in the cool of the day and in the midnight hour, when the owl and the nightingale sing their songs of peace. Yes, my child, my little one, I Am that I Am. I am Alpha and Omega, your beginning and your end. I am the author and the finisher of your life eternal. Listen to me. Don't listen to the false prophets of the age. Listen to My heart. I love and I care for you very deeply. By my very life's blood, I have claimed you for My own. Now be at peace. Trust me. I know you cannot see Me, but You have My Word, My will and My bond with you. Believe My Word, and someday, we will be with each other forever in My arms of love."

**Scriptures:**

Hear my prayer, O Lord,
And let my cry come to You.
Do not hide Your face from me in the day of my trouble;
Incline Your ear to me;
In the day that I call, answer me speedily.
For my days are consumed like smoke,
And my bones are burned like a hearth.

Psalm 102:1-3

Call upon Me in the day of trouble, I will deliver you,
and you shall glorify Me."

Psalm 50:15

# God, Where Were You?

God,
Where were You when I needed You?
I cried.
I begged.
I pleaded.
I called out Your holy, precious name.
Didn't You understand
how deeply I was hurting?
Why God, why did You abandon me
in my deepest hour of need?
Lord, don't You understand
that my guts were wrenched in the pain
of living in this world with all its sorrows?
Here am I, oh God, my king, as I call out to You,
deep to deep,
heart to heart,
life to life,
soul to soul.
Now answer me please, Lord Jesus,
my only hope.
Rescue me, oh God Almighty,
Keeper of my heart,
and all that I am.

I am your Lord,
your God,
your Savior,
the great I Am,
Almighty God.
By my very blood
I knew even on the cross
the pain that you would encounter.
Do you truly believe that I abandoned you

In your deepest hour of need?
Don't you know?
Don't you know?
Don't you understand My ways?
Don't you know?
Don't you know
that I am not ten thousand miles away from you?
I am not around on the other side of the world hiding from you?
I live in you,
*in* you,
within your heart.
From the very first moment you called Me into your heart
I recreated you.
Now you are a new creation,
full of light,
life,
and peace eternal.
You are Mine and I am yours
throughout all eternity.
I rescued you from
death,
hell,
and the grave,
the schemes of the enemy.
I brought you instead into light, life eternal
with Me forevermore.
Don't you believe My word when I tell you
I will be with you always, even to the end of the age?
When you cry the tears,
I feel the pain.
My tears, they do flow.
Come to Me, my little one,
My precious child.
Come to Me, and I will give you rest.
Come to Me, and I will give you peace.
Come to Me, and I will give you joy in the midst of the storm
from My loving hands of mercy and grace

forevermore until eternity passes away
into the distant sands of time.
I will,
I will,
I will
be with you to comfort you,
protect you,
to care for you.
I will never let go of your hand.

# Lord, I Call Out to You

My dearest Lord, God and Savior,
I call out to You
as one calling out to You
in a very present time of danger.
I call out to You
as one calling out in the wilderness.
I thirst for Your Word,
Your presence.
I hunger for Your name,
Your love,
Your gentleness,
Your kindness.
I cry the tears of pain,
I cry a tear of sorrow.
I cry a pain of
sadness,
emptiness,
and hopelessness.
Please, please remember me.
Forgive me,
rescue me,
for my heart has been broken,
crushed,
destroyed by the weight,
the trouble,
the grief of this world.
My dearest Lord God and Savior,
I call out to You.
My mind has been entrapped
by the enemy's plans and schemes.
He has entrapped my mind.
My heart is troubled.
Mmy heart is in despair.

Break the chains,
free my heart,
my mind
from the bands,
the torment,
the fear,
the anguish
that camps out from within,
ready to strike me
with the final blow of destruction.
My dearest Lord God and Savior,
though the world,
the enemy,
the troubles of this world may surround me
to destroy my very being,
I will trust in You.
I will wait for You.
I will rest in the strength of the Lord my God,
for the Lord my God
is my light and my salvation,
my peace,
my joy in the times of trouble
from here to eternity past.

# My Daughter

My daughter,
My friend,
My child,
do you not know that I am the Lord your God,
your hope,
your peace,
your life,
your very next breath?
Do you not know
that you are the candle and I am the flame?
You are the flower,
I am the rain.
You are the instrument,
I am the musician.
Between the two of us we have harmony,
we sing a new song.
Without you there is no music in My heart.
Without Me, there is no life.
How can you have music without a song?
How can you have a song without music?
My daughter,
My friend,
My child,
I am the Lord your God,
the Good Shepherd.
I feel your pain,
I see the hurting anguish in the middle of the night
that cries out to me in the torment,
the loneliness that chokes your loving, caring heart.
I am your King,
your Hope,
your Peace,
your Life,

your very next breath.
I am the author of your very next heartbeat.
I am the Good Shepherd, and I love you.
My heart, it calls out to you, it searches for you.
I will not let you go.
I will not let you go.
Wherever you go
I will love you.
Wherever you go
I will care for you.
If you call out to Me in the cool of the day,
I will hear you.
If your heart cries out to Me in the middle of the night,
I will answer you with kindness,
mercy,
grace,
and compassion.
Yes, My child, come to Me and I will love you,
I will shelter you from the storms of life,
I will give you rest.

# The Cry of the Heart

The cry of the heart,
it speaks in the middle of the night
with pain and travail.
Where are you, God?
Where are you?
The cry of the heart,
it speaks in the middle of the night
with confusion and despair.
I do not understand, Lord.
I do not understand.
The cry of the heart,
it speaks in the middle of the night
in desperation and want.
Do you not care?
Do you not hear me?
Are you not the God of all living things?
Are you not the God of all there is, will be, and ever was throughout
the ages?

"My child, have you not known?
Have you not heard?
The everlasting God,
the Lord,
the Creator of the ends of the earth,
neither faints nor is weary.
His understanding is unsearchable.
He gives power to the weak,
and to those who have no might
He increases strength.
Even the youths shall faint and be weary
and the young men shall utterly fall,
but those who wait on the Lord
shall renew their strength;

they shall mount up with wings like eagles,
they shall run and not be weary,
they shall walk and not be faint." *
Have you not heard Me crying as you cry,
hurting when you hurt?
In you I live and I breathe.
In you I am touched
by the brokenness of your heart
as I have carried you through the midst of the storm.
I am the cool breeze that blows the easterly winds
to comfort your heated brow.
I am
the rustling of the wind.
I am
the one who commands the nightingale
to sing the song of the night with love and compassion.
I Am that I Am.
You were created for My good pleasure.
I am yours, and you are Mine.
You were bought by my sacrifice,
My blood,
My compassion,
My very life.
Trust Me, My child.
I do hear your cry .
Trust Me throughout all eternity,
for I will never let go of your hand.


* Isaiah 40:28-31

# Who Am I God?

Who am I, God? I am Your servant. I am Yours to command. I am the one who calls upon You in the midst of the storm and You hear my cry.

Who am I, my loving Savior? I am the one who was in torment, and pain, and You heard my cry. You set me upon high, You dressed my mental and physical wounds with Your love and compassion.

You are the one who ripped off and destroyed the chains from the enemy, never to be seen again. Who am I, my loving Jesus? I am the one who seeks You daily. My life and my hope are met by You in all compassion as You fulfill my needs by the word of Your power. Who am I, oh God? I am Your child, Your servant, yours from here to eternity past. I hear, and I obey.

**Scriptures:**

Know that the Lord, He is God;
It is He that has made us, and not we ourselves;
We are His people and the sheep of His pasture.

Psalm 100:3

To everything there is a season,
A time to every purpose under the heaven:

Ecclesiastes 3:1

Fear not, for I am with you;
Be not dismayed, for I am your God.
I will strengthen you,
Yes, I will help you,
I will uphold you with My righteous right hand.

Isaiah 41:10

He gives power to the weak,
And to those who have no might He increases strength.

Isaiah 40:29

# I Am the Instrument of the Lord

I am the instrument of the Lord.
I am the singer.
I sing the song.
I am the singer.
I sing the song of love.
I am the singer.
I sing the song of the Lord my God.
I am the singer.
I sing the song of
praise,
glory,
honor,
and respect unto Your holy, precious, name.
I am the singer.
I sing the mighty song of worship
unto the Lord my God.
I am the singer.
I am the warrior.
I am the child of the Most High God.
I am the singer.
I sing the song of high praise,
to do battle against
the enemy,
the dragon,
the keeper,
the holder of all lies and deceit.
I am the victorious one
through the blood of the Lamb
and by the word of my testimony.
I am the champion.
I am the warrior.
I am the keeper of His mighty name
as I glory in the holy name of the Lord my God,

my King,
my source,
my supply,
my abundance.
I die to myself.
It is by You, and You alone,
that I breathe and I have life.
I sing the song of praise,
honor,
worship,
and glory
unto my mighty King, the Lion of Judah,
The Holy One of God,
The King of kings,
and Lord of lords.
Yes, my precious Lord God and Savior,
by Your precious blood,
by Your mighty hand of righteousness,
love,
and peace,
I surrender willfully unto Your command.
I say unto You my loving, caring King,
I am the singer.
I sing the song to praise you,
to worship you,
forevermore,
forevermore,
forevermore,
unto all eternity and beyond!

# Who Am I?

Who am I, oh Lord
but a whisper in the wind,
a grain of sand along the beach,
a drop of water in the endless sea?
Who am I, Lord?
by His spoken word
I am a child of the Most High God.
Spoken,
created
for His good pleasure.
I am a child of the Most High God
clothed by His glory,
lifted from the pit by his blood,
by His power,
by His majesty.
I am the keeper of His word,
to carry on what He has decreed,
called to be in the earth for now and forever.
I believe,
I trust,
I obey,
I decree His holy, holy word.
For His Word is truth.
I speak His Word,
I was created by His Word,
for His Word shall accomplish
that for which it has been sent.
His Word does not come back void.
Who am I?
I am a child of the Most High God.
Keeper, proclaimer, spokesman
of and for His holy, precious Word,
for His Word is truth.

Who am I?
I am one who has been clothed, robed
in garments of righteousness,
peace,
and joy.
By His very hand,
by His blood,
by His spoken Word.
Who am I?
I am a child of the Most High God,
Jesus Christ,
the Son of the Most High God!

**Scripture:**

For I know the thoughts that I think toward you, says the Lord, thoughts of peace and not of evil, to give you a future and a hope. Then you will call upon Me and go and pray to Me, and I will listen to you. And you will seek Me and find Me, when you search for Me with all your heart.

Jeremiah 29:11-13

# Who Are You, God?

Who are you, Lord, but the author and finisher of my very life? Who are you, Lord, but the creator of earth and sky, wind and rain? From the clay of which you also created me do I exist. Who are you, Lord? You are my life, my Lord, my God, my comfort, my joy. You are the One who constantly assures me in troubled times that everything will be all right. When I cry tears like a river, You are there for me.

So, who are you, Lord? You are the ocean so vast. You are the sky above, the earth below. Creator of all that is or ever will be.

Who are you? Remember the tears that I cried when my mother died? You were there. Remember all the times when I fell down as a little child and skinned my knees? You were there.

Yes, my Lord God and Savior, who are You? You are life and you are love in the midst of the storm. You are hope and you are peace. Oh, hold me close my loving Jesus, for I am Yours and You are mine.

**Scripture:**

I am the bread of life.

John 6:48

I am the good shepherd. The good shepherd gives His life for the sheep.

John 10:11

Heal me, O Lord, and I shall be healed;
Save me, and I shall be saved,
For You are my praise.

Jeremiah 17:14

I am the Alpha and the Omega, the Beginning and the End, the First and the Last.

Revelation 22:13

I, Jesus have sent My angel to testify to you these things in the churches. I am the Root and the Offspring of David, the Bright and Morning Star.

Revelation 22:16

I am the Alpha and the Omega, the Beginning and the End," says the Lord, "who is and who was and who is to come, the Almighty."

Revelation 1:8

In the beginning was the Word, and the Word was with God, and the Word was God. He was in the beginning with God. All things were made through Him, and without Him nothing was made. In Him was life, and the life was the light of men. And the light shines in the darkness, and the darkness did not comprehend it.

John1:1-5

For unto us a Child is born,
Unto us a Son is given;
And the government will be upon His shoulder.
And His name will be called
Wonderful, Counselor, Mighty God,
Everlasting Father, Prince of Peace.

Isaiah 9:6

Lord, how they have increased who trouble me!
Many are they who rise up against me.
Many are they who say of me,
"There is no help for him in God."

But you, o Lord, are a shield for me,
My glory and the One who lifts up my head.
I cried to the Lord with my voice,
And He heard me from His holy hill.

Psalm 3:1-4

Hear me when I call, O God of my righteousness!
You have relieved me in my distress;
Have mercy on me, and hear my prayer.

Psalm 4:1

# God Is

God is
a fresh ray of sunlight for the chilled morning
to bring every living creature warmth and comfort.

God is
the love of your first puppy dog.

God is
the kindness of how you help others in need.

God is
being truthful no matter how unworthy people are to you.

God is
being happy and carefree over simply being alive.

God is
the beauty of a child running through a meadow of freshly grown
flowers and seeing the joy of this child discovering nature and its
boundless beauty.

God is many things,
but all beauty is love, a gift from God.

# God of Love

God of love,
God of mercy,
God of grace,
God of gentleness,
God of kindness,
God of peace,
God of joy,
God of light,
God of healing.
By blood and steel,
the cat-o'-nine-tails,
You were whipped.
You were beaten.
You were punished.
You were despised.
You were spat upon.
By blood and steel,
the cross of death,
You were nailed.
You were scorned.
You were bruised.
You were stabbed.
You were cursed.
God of love,
gentleness,
kindness,
mercy,
and grace eternal.
You, and you alone
paid the price for all of my sins.
By Your blood, I have been saved.
By Your blood, I have been made whole.
By Your blood, I am complete.

You gave us peace,
we gave You pain.
You gave us life,
we gave You death.
You gave us healing,
we gave You the cat-o'-nine-tails,
torture,
and pain.
Through blood and steel,
You were the bridge to our salvation.
Through it all,
You were there for us.
We rejected You,
You loved us.
We buried You in the tomb,
You paid the price to buy us back.
You suffered
death,
hell,
and the grave.
We gained
heaven,
the kingdom of God,
eternal salvation.
As the blood flowed,
our sins were washed away into the sea of nevermore,
the oceans of the past eternal.
Through blood and steel the holy sacrifice,
through Your blood and pain
I have been freed from this world.
I thank you Jesus, my Lord,
for You are my bridge to life eternal
forevermore, until the end of eternity past!
Amen!

# He Is God

He is good.
He is kind.
He is loving.
He is compassionate.
He is God.
He is caring.
He is gentle.
He is life.
He is joy.
He is God.
He is the Mighty Creator.
He is Elohim.
He is Jehovah.
He is our Redeemer.
He is God.
He is Emmanuel.
He is our Wonderful Counselor.
He is our Mighty God.
He is our Everlasting Father
He is God.
He is the Lion of Judah.
He is the Morning Star.
He Is the Word of God.
He is the King of Kings and Lord of Lords.
He is God.
He Is Jehovah-Tsidkenu, Jehovah Our Righteousness.
He Is Jehovah-M'kaddesh, Jehovah Who Sanctifies.
He Is Jehovah-Shalom, Jehovah Is Peace.
He Is Jehovah-Shammah, Jehovah Is There.
He Is God.
He Is Jehovah-Rophe, Jehovah Heals.
He Is Jehovah-Jireh, Jehovah's Provision Shall be Seen.
He Is Jehovah-Nissi, Jehovah My Banner.

He Is Jehovah-Rohi, Jehovah My Shepherd.
He Is God.
He Is Lord.
He Is Savior.
He is eternal.
He is my friend.
He is God.
He is the creator of all that is good, holy, and pure.
He is pure of heart,
of love,
the eternal sacrifice.
He is my refuge,
my fortress,
my hedge of protection.
He is the Alpha and the Omega,
the First and the Last,
The Beginning and the End.
He is my Jesus Christ,
the Son of the Living God.
He is my home eternal!
He is my God!

# He Is Lord

He is.
He Is Lord.
He Is Savior.
He Is Master.
He Is God Almighty.
He Is the Creator Elohim.
He Is Jehovah My Reedemer.
He Is the Great I Am.
He is Alpha, my beginning.
He is Omega, my end.
He is my peace in the midst of the storm.
He is my hope in times of trouble.
He is the keeper of my heart.
He is the One who gives me life.
He is my hope in the turmoil of this world.
He is my joy in the morning.
He is love in perilous times,
the champion of my heart and life.
He is my king.
He is my source.
He is my supply.
He is my abundance.
He is the bearer of all sins.
He is my everything I need in this life
and all throughout eternity!
Amen!

# I Am the Author of Your Life

I am the author,
You are the pen.
I am the author,
You are the paper.
I am the author,
You are the story.
I am the author,
I am your life.
I am the author,
I am your peace.
I am the author,
I am your hope.
I am the author,
you are the clay.
I am the author,
I am the sculptor,
you are My creation.
I am yours and you are Mine.
I am the way,
the truth,
and the life.
I am the one who is ever-present,
always loving,
always caring,
always blessing.
I am Alpha and Omega,
your beginning and ending of your existence.
I Am that I Am.
I am your present time of peace
in the midst of the storm.
I am your future,
the One who will dry the tears of yesterdays past.
I am the keeper of your heart,

the One who will bless you
with the dawning of your future.
I am the author and finisher of your first heartbeat,
your last breath.
Yes, I am your king,
the author of your life.
I am yours, and you are Mine.
You were bought with a price,
By the blood of Jesus Christ,
the Son of the Living God.
I will walk with you in the cool of the day.
I will talk with you in the evening.
I Am that I Am.
I love you.
I need you.
I care for you.
I will be with you forevermore
until the setting of the sun,
the dawning of the morning,
the eve of eternity past.

# I Am the Carpenter's Son

I am the Carpenter's Son,
the Lion of Judah,
the Rose of Sharon,
the Bright and Morning Star.

I am the Carpenter's Son,
the God of mercy,
the God of grace,
the God of love.

I am the Carpenter's Son,
the Prince of Peace,
the God of hope,
the God of joy unspeakable.

I am the Carpenter's Son,
the great I Am,
the creator of all there is and ever shall be,
the redeemer of all I am and what I shall become.

I am the Carpenter's Son,
the healer of broken hearts,
the Savior of the world,
the mighty One.

I am the Carpenter's son,
the adopted one who has been bought by the price,
by His very blood.
By His suffering,
by His pain,
By His stripes,
By His sacrifice,
By His broken body.

Yes, my friend,
I am the Carpenter's son,
by His blood
that kissed the ground with compassion,
as he poured out His life,
not thinking of Himself.
He left glory to win me back,
to pay the price which I could never pay.
I am the Carpenter's son,
by His blood,
by His might,
by His power,
by His love,
by His mercy,
by His grace,
by His holy, holy, name,
by the word of His power.
Yes, I am the Carpenter's son.
I am His, and He is mine.
He is my Father,
I am His son.
Forevermore and throughout all eternity!

# I Am Yours

I Am
the great and the mighty One,
the holy, the just, and the fair One.

I Am
your Life.
Without Me you will not survive.

I Am
Your King,
Your source,
your supply,
and your abundance.
The One who is ever-present.
Always loving,
always caring,
always blessing.

I Am
the One of today,
tomorrow,
and of yesterday.
I will always be there for you,
For I am your God!

# I Remember

I remember
that You are the Way, the truth, and the life.
I remember
that You are the great I Am.
I remember
that You are the one who is ever-present in my life.
Always loving,
always caring,
always blessing.
I remember
that You are my refuge,
my strength,
my rampart,
my strong tower in a very present time of danger.
Yes, You are
my Lord,
my God,
my king,
my Savior,
the keeper of all that I am,
for You are my God.
Yes, You are my
Jehovah,
Elohim,
my redeemer
with Your very blood,
my creator
by Your mighty power.
You are
the great I am,
my peace in the midst of the storm!

# The Author of Life

I Am that I Am
I Am
the reason you live.
I Am
the author of your life.
I Am
the writer's pen, you are the paper.
I Am
the writer, you are the story.
I Am
the rain, you are the flower, you need me to survive.
I Am
steel,
you are the magnet,
you are drawn to Me by My loving touch.
I Am
the potter, you are the clay.
I have formed you with My hands
out of the dust of the earth.
I have breathed the breath of life into your nostrils
to make you a living creature.
I have paid the price for you.
I have spilled My blood so you could be free from sin.
You are free from the torment of the enemy's pleasure--
death,
hell,
and the grave.
Your destination is heaven,
a gift from God.
You are a citizen of heaven eternal
because you have accepted Jesus Christ,
the Son of the living God,
as your Lord God and Savior.

Yes, I am the writer's pen,
the author of your life.
You are the piece of paper.
I write My laws of love,
peace,
joy,
hope,
and life eternal
upon your heart forevermore.
I will be with you to comfort you,
and to give you peace.
My law is love.
I freely surrender Myself to you as your king.
I will be yours and you will be Mine
forevermore,
forevermore,
forevermore.

# The King

I Am, I said,
not of today,
tomorrow,
or of yesterday,
but the One of all eternity.
I know your beginning and your end.
I see through the sands of eternity past.
I Am that I Am.
I see your heart,
your mind,
your body,
your soul,
your spirit.
I am all-seeing,
all-knowing,
for I am your God,
the King of Glory.
The Author and Finisher of your life!

# Who Are You?

Who are you, God,
but the mighty One?
The strong One.
The God of Peace.
The God of Love.
The God of Hope.
The God of Patience.
The Great I Am,
my mighty God Emmanuel.
God With Us,
the Rose of Sharon,
the Prince of Peace,
the Lion of Judah.
You are my God,
from everlasting to all eternity.
You are my king,
the God of Abraham,
Issac,
and Jacob.
You are Jesus Christ,
the Son of the living God.

# Praise Him!

In this life and beyond, I will praise you, for You are the reason I live and I breathe. Can I take credit for singing praises unto your holy name? No, You created my tongue. Can I take credit for playing instruments to lift you up upon high? No, I cannot, for you are the One who created the fingers to perform and play the music that I play for You and only You. Can I take credit for writing a book of love and proclaiming your holy name? Again, I proclaim, the answer is no. You are the Author and Finisher of my very last breath. You are the Holy One of God who has created the brain, the instrument of your design. So you see, my loving Jesus, my Lord God and Savior, it is You that is worthy to be praised unto the highest mountain, even unto the sky above and beyond. Yes, I do love You my loving Jesus, for You are my eternal King from here to eternity past.

**Scriptures:**

Make a joyful shout to the Lord, all you lands!
Serve the Lord with gladness;
Come before His presence with singing.

Psalm 100:1-2

Blessed be the God and Father of our Lord Jesus Christ, who has blessed us with every spiritual blessing in the heavenly places in Christ, Just as He choose us in Him before the foundation of the world, that we should be holy and without blame before Him in love, having predestined us to adoption as sons by Jesus Christ to Himself, according to the good pleasure of His will, To the praise of the glory of His grace, by which He made us accepted in the beloved.

Ephesians 1:3-6

# Anchor of My Soul

Jesus Christ, the Son of the living God, anchor of my soul.
Hosanna!
Jesus Christ, the Son of the living God, my life.
Hosanna!
Jesus Christ, the Son of the living God, My king.
Hosanna!
Jesus Christ, anchor of my soul, my life, my king.
Hosanna!
Jesus Christ my loving master, reason to live.
Hosanna!
When this old world rushes in like a flood,
I worship,
I worship,
I will worship,
for the Lord inhabits the praises of His people.
Jesus Christ, my anchor, my life, my peace, I need You.
I surrender my vessel, this ship of clay, flesh,
perishable to the touch.
This ship of mortal materials,
fashioned by Your hands, is sinking.
Come quickly, please, God, my creator Elohim,
my only hope, my redeemer true.
Please, oh God of my heart, my mind, my body,
touch me with Your presence, Your peace, Your loving hands.
Make me complete in You, the way that only You can do.
Hosanna to the king of glory.
Hosanna in the highest.
The king of hope, my redemptive peace
in the whirlwinds of time eternal.
In the midst of the storms of life I will praise You.

Through all the storms of forevermore, I will be Yours.
I will worship.
I will thank You for all time.
Hosanna!
Hosanna!
Hosanna in the highest!
Amen!

# Behold

Behold!
Lord God Almighty, king and ruler of the universe.
Are You not the author of my next breath?
Behold!
Are You not the keeper of my very next heartbeat?
Behold!
Are You not the Creator of all living things?
Behold!
Are You not the One
who spilled Your very life's blood
as it kissed the ground with joy
for the salvation of all mankind?
My dearest Lord God Almighty,
Creator,
Elohim.
If this is all true,
then tell me, tell me, tell me true,
why do they not believe?
If You are truly the
Redeemer,
Jehovah,
the victorious One,
the Holy One,
the God of all love,
the God of all peace,
then why, oh why, do men not believe?
Why do they mock You,
spit on Your holy Word,
and say there is no God?
Why do the people take from Your holy word
and say that You were just a good man?
My dearest Lord,
as for me and my house, we are the victors

because of Your name.
In my house You are King.
In my house You are God.
In my house we serve, honor, and respect You,
and only You.
From this day forward,
You have heard my words of praise
from the very depths of my heart.
You have heard Your child,
the one who You have saved
by Your bodily sacrifice,
and from the shedding of Your blood.
If nobody else will speak it, then I will.
You are
Lord,
God,
and Savior.
Thank You, oh Lord of my
heart,
my mind,
my body,
soul,
and spirit.
I surrender.
I surrender.
I am Yours,
I am Yours, forevermore,
unto the very last day of eternity.
And I will be Your servant,
to proclaim the holy precious Word of God,
the gospel which brought me
peace in the midst of the storms of my life.
This word I speak to you who do not believe:
"I proclaim, I testify, that Jesus Christ loves you,
as He is calling out to you in the midnight hour
with His love,
his compassion,

his blood,
and His gift of peace,
and eternal life forever."
Time is short!
Jesus calls out to You only in this lifetime saying,
"Behold, I stand at the door and knock.
If anyone hears My voice and opens the door,
I will come in to him and dine with him,
and he with Me.
To him who overcomes
I will grant to sit with Me on My throne,
as I also overcame and sat down with My father on His throne."*
Jesus is waiting.
Are You ready?


*Revelation 3:20-21

# My God Is My Lighthouse

My God
is my lighthouse.
My God
is my lighthouse of peace.
My God
is my lighthouse of hope.
My God
is my lighthouse of mercy.
My God
is my lighthouse of grace.
My God
is my lighthouse of joy.
My God
is my lighthouse of love.
My God
is my lighthouse in times of trouble.
My God
is my lighthouse,
my deliverer in the midst of the storm.
My God
is my lighthouse,
my anchor,
to sustain me from the perils of tomorrow's sorrow.
My God is my God.
My God is my king.
My God is my shelter.
My God is my refuge.
My God is my rose of Sharon.
My God is my Lion of Judah.
My God is my light in the darkness,
a very present help in times of trouble.
My God is my
redeemer and creator.

My God is my
Alpha and Omega,
my beginning and my end.
My God is my song,
a song of
love,
joy,
peace,
hope,
and love.
My God is my lighthouse
to guide me into the kingdom of God,
my eternal home,
from here to eternity past.
forevermore,
forevermore,
forevermore!

# On the Other Side of Midnight

On the other side of midnight,
the whispering winds, they call out to me.
My heart, it cries.
My soul, it soars like the clouds above
which bring forth the tears of heaven,
mountains high,
valleys low.
So is my life.
Good times,
bad times,
joy and peace,
they all make up this life in which we live.
The sands of time reach out to tomorrow,
searching for the hope of eternal peace.
It is your way that I strive for, oh God,
for You are the Way, the Truth and the Life.
You are my rampart,
my shield,
my wings of love,
safety and protection.
You are my all in all,
the very essence of my being.
You are my sun in the morning,
my moon and stars at night.
By Your precious blood, You are my life eternal,
my glorious king.
You are
my Lion of Judah, the great I Am.
You are
My Lion of Judah, the Prince of Peace.
You are
My Lion of Judah,
my salvation, my hope.
But most of all, You are my creator, redeemer,
Jesus Christ, the Son of the Living God.

# Shall I Tell You?

Shall I tell you
about my king,
my Lord God and Savior,
the great I Am,
the Lion of Judah,
the Rose of Sharon?
Shall I tell you
of His love of man?
Shall I tell you
of my mighty God Elohim, my creator?
How He created Adam with His very hand,
spoke His word upon him,
and breathed His life-giving breath into his nostrils?
Shall I tell you
how God had mercy and compassion upon His creation,
saw his loneliness,
and gave him a mate of love, gentleness, and care.
Shall I tell you
of His redemptive plan.
My loving, saving Savior who, on His own accord,
spilled His very blood to save man?
Shall I tell you
how that he was the Lamb for the slaughter?
Shall I tell you
of His endless love for you and me?
Shall I tell you
we were bought with and by a price
by the eternal, loving blood of Jesus Christ,
the anointed One?
The Holy One,
the redeemer of all man kind?
He is Lord,
He is God,

He is Savior,
the creator and finisher of my life,
my very next heartbeat.
He is the author of my next breath.
Yes, he is Lord,
He is God,
He is Savior,
the great I Am,
outside of time.
The great I Am,
always there for me.
The great I Am,
ever-present with His love and care for me
from here to eternity.
This is my God.

# The Holy One

To You, my Holy One,
the God of Israel,
the One of glory and majesty.
The Lord,
Master,
Savior,
and King of
Abraham,
Issac,
and Jacob.
You are to be
praised,
glorified, and
honored,
for You are the seed of hope,
the seed of peace,
the seed of eternity.
I pledge my allegiance to You,
for You were the Lamb for the slaughter,
Jehovah Redeemer,
Elohim Creator,
my beginning,
my end.
You are God Almighty,
the great I Am.
Through your blood I have
my hope,
my peace,
my salvation,
my very essence of being,
from this point in time into all eternity.
Praise God forever.
Amen!

# The Names of God Be Praised

Are you not the whispering of the wind in the cool of the day?
Are you not the dew of the morning,
the tears of heaven above?
Are you not the burning bush
that Moses proclaimed to be God from up on high?
Are you not the mighty creator, Elohim, of all living things?
Are you not the Holy One of God?
The redeemer, Jehovah,
the One who shed His precious blood so I may be saved?
Are you not Jehovah-Tsidkenu, "Jehovah our Righteousness"
Are you not Jehovah-M'kaddesh, "Jehovah who Sanctifies"
Are you not Jehovah-Shalom, "Jehovah is Peace"
Are you not Jehovah-Shammah, "Jehovah is There"
Are you not Jehovah-Rophe, "Jehovah Heals"
Are you not Jehovah-Jireh, "Jehovah's Provision Shall be Seen"
Are you not Jehovah-Nissi, "Jehovah my Banner"
Are you not Jehovah-Rohi, "Jehovah my Shepherd"
Yes, I proclaim who You are, my God.
You are my all in all.
You are life and you are love in the midst of the storm.
You are my peace in the midst of the raging ocean waves.
You are my salvation in the rushing rivers of my soul.
You are my Savior.
The One who rescues me
even before the tides of time try to destroy me,
to sweep me away into the vastness of desolation.
Yes, oh yes, my King,
You are Lord,
You are God,
You are Savior,
You are the Lion of Judah.
You are Alpha and Omega,
the beginning and the end.

You are the morning star of glory, and peace.
You are the Holy One of whom I do worship.
I glory in You from the highest tower proclaiming you to be
my King,
my Lord,
my God,
the very essence of my life.
You and You alone are my king.
You are the reason I live and I breathe.
Forever You will be my king,
unto the ending of eternity past.
Forevermore my praise and worship will go out to You.
For You are my God!

# Prayer and Proclamation

I stand on the Word of God daily. I proclaim to Him personally that He is my source, my supply, and my abundance. Without Him I am nothing. He is my beacon of light in the midst of the storm. He is my light in the darkness. He is my ever-present help for now and forever. His Word is the sail on my ship. He leads, guides, and directs me into His plans for my life. I don't want my way. All I want is His will, His plan, His way - *His* way only. When I live without His Word, it's like I am in a vast desert without water or the bread of life that sustains me daily. As for me and my house, I choose to live by every word that proceeds out of the mouth of God Almighty - my king, my Lord, my Savior, my friend. Jesus is the light in the darkness. Jesus is my all in all from here to eternity and beyond.

**Scriptures:**

Your word I have hidden in my heart,
That I may not sin against You.

Psalm 119:11

And if it seems evil to you to serve the Lord, choose yourselves this day whom you will serve, whether the gods which your fathers served that were on the other side of the River, or the gods of the Amorites, in whose land you dwell. But as for me and my house, we will serve the Lord."

Joshua 24:15

Not that anyone has seen the Father, except He who is from God; He has seen the Father. Most assuredly, I say to you, he who believes in Me has eternal life. I am the bread of life.

John 6:46-48

# The Prayer

Father God,
I come before You in the name of Jesus,
the name that is above all other names.
For You and You alone are my Lord, my God, my Savior.
I pray for all my family members.
I also pray for my pastor, his family, my church,
and all the churches all around the world.
I pray for them to have
peace,
safety,
protection,
health,
and well-being.
And I pray for a legion of
warring,
ministering,
healing,
and protecting angels
to be encamped all around them.
I pray for the peace of Jerusalem
and the United States of America.
I pray for the leaders of the land to make Godly decisions
through Your wisdom, knowledge, and understanding
for the sake of Your people.
I pray for revival in the land to be upheld by Your righteous right hand
of mercy and grace.
I do pray, oh God, for
Your way,
Your will,
and Your plan
to be done and established.
In Jesus Christ's name I do humbly and respectfully pray,
Amen.

# The Proclamation

---

We are the head and not the tail,
above and not beneath.
We are blessed in the city,
blessed in the country,
blessed coming in
and blessed going out.
We are like trees planted by streams of water,
whose leaf does not wither,
and whatever our hands touch will prosper.
We have abundance and no lack.
The blessings of God, they overtake us,
for we are healthy, wealthy and wise.
We have Godly
wisdom,
knowledge,
and understanding.
We are always at the right place at the right time.
We are blessed of God in every area of our life.
For we are children of the Most High God.
Amen.

**Scripture:**

Therefore, brethren, having boldness to enter the
Holiest by the blood of Jesus, by a new and living
way which He consecrated for us, through the veil,
that is, His flesh, and having a High Priest over the
house of God, let us draw near with a true heart in
full assurance of faith, having our hearts sprinkled
from an evil conscience and our bodies washed with
pure water.

Hebrews 10:19-22

# Redeemed by the Blood!

No longer, my little ones. No longer will we have to sacrifice the animals. The tender lamb for your eternal sacrifice. The Lamb for the slaughter has come. He has paid the price with His blood the sacrifice of His own body.

The Holy Spirit has raised Jesus our king from the grave. How wonderful, how great it is. He has arisen. You are free, free at last because of the things He has done for you and me. It is finished! The second Adam, Jesus Christ, the Son of the living God, our King of kings, Lord of lords, has come. He has secured our salvation with His loving blood upon the cross, upon the hill of honor, calvary, where you and I died and were raised from the grave. He paid the price. He took our place so we could live throughout all eternity with Him.

It is finished!
It is finished!
It is finished!

**Scriptures:**

Seeing then that we have a great High Priest who has passed through the heavens, Jesus the Son of God, let us hold fast our confession. For we do not have a High Priest who cannot sympathize with our weakness, but was in all points tempted as we are, yet without sin. Let us therefore come boldly to the throne of grace, that we may obtain mercy and find grace to help in time of need.

Hebrews 4:14-16

There is therefore now no condemnation to those who are in Christ Jesus, who do not walk according to the flesh, but according to the spirit. For the law of the Spirit of life in Christ Jesus has made me free from the law of sin and death. For what the law could not do in that it was weak through the flesh, God did by sending His own Son in the likeness of sinful flesh, on account of sin: He condemned sin in the flesh, that the righteous requirement of the law might be fulfilled in us who do not walk according to the flesh but according to the Spirit. For those who live according to the flesh set their minds on the things of the flesh, but those who live according to the Spirit, the things of the Spirit. For to be carnally minded is death, but to be spiritually minded is life and peace. Because the carnal mind is enmity against God; for it is not subject to the law of God, nor indeed can be. So then, those who are in the flesh cannot please God.

But you are not in the flesh but in the spirit, if indeed the Spirit of God dwells in you. Now if anyone does not have the Spirit of Christ, he is not His. And if Christ is in you, the body is dead because of sin, but the Spirit is life because of righteousness. But if the Spirit of Him who raised Jesus from the dead dwells in you, He who raised Christ from the dead will also give life to your mortal bodies through his Spirit who dwells in you.

Romans 8:1-11

# Adam

Adam,
you had it all.
Then came the fall.
You no longer hear the call of the Master,
nor do you feel the touch of the Creator's hands
through your spirit.
No longer the gentle walks in the cool of the morning,
nor the evening mist so peaceful and true.
Your spirit is now dead.
No more daily fellowship with the One that you have loved.
You have been taken away,
held captive,
abducted by the evil one
with the schemes of that old dragon,
the devil,
the father of all lies.
Now only the fleshly mind remains,
governed by Lucifer the evil angel,
the king of
death,
hell,
and the grave.
Now, only remembrance of the glory past.
The days did not last.

Oh Adam, your rib, flesh of your flesh,
your companion of the ages past,
mother of your firstborn.
Eve, the light of beauty, creation of God Eternal.
Therein were you both deceived in the garden of Eden.
The angel of beauty, of light, that old serpent,
deceiver of the nations all of mankind,
has been judged for all eternity

with the sin of pride and high treason
against the most Holy God.

Behold!
My children, take heart,
be at peace,
for your Redeemer, the Second Adam,
lives and breathes in the person of Jesus Christ,
the Son of the Living God.
For by the tears and love of your redeemer,
your champion,
the victorious One,
the morning star,
Emmanuel,
the lion of Judah,
the King of Kings and Lord of Lords
has fought for you, has won you back to himself
once and for all times.
By His blood, by His holy, precious blood,
He surrendered up His broken body,
as the blood flowed, spilled,
kissing the ground gently, softly, with all compassion.
Behold!
My little ones, I am the good shepherd.
I have won you back.
I have the keys to your heart once again.
Now come to me freely so I may give you
rivers of living water,
peace in the midst of the storm.
I will give you rest.
Now come to Me,
come to Me, My little children
so that we may once again walk together
in the cool of the morning and in the evening mist
so peaceful and true.
Here am I, your King,
your Lord,

your God,
your redeemer.
I am waiting patiently for you to come to me.
It is truly your decision.
Now walk with Me,
walk with Me,
once again,
hand in hand throughout all eternity.
For I am forevermore your God,
And you shall forevermore be My children.

# I Paid the Price

I cried the tears, I felt the pain,
as I paid the price for you.
I cried the tears, I felt the pain
as My blood poured out and kissed the ground
with all love and compassion.
Yes, I cried the tears, I felt the pain
as I called out your precious name.
Yes, I paid the price.
I cannot do it twice.
My child,
it's time to come home, little one.
It's time to come home.
The tears, the scars,
they still speak,
they will always search for you.
They still remain as I call out your name.
The pain is gone.
I paid the price.
I'm waiting with open arms.
Come to me little one, come to me.
Do you not know,
can you not see,
The precious love that I have for you?
Who will you listen to,
mankind, or My heart that cries out to you
as a mother who has lost her child?
Yes, I cried the tears,
I felt the pain as I paid the price for you.
I call out your name now, my precious child,
in the midnight hour.
Please come home.
I have prepared a place for you,
for I am your Lord Jesus Christ,
your Savior,
your love,
your life.

# My God Is a Consuming Fire

I am, I said,
your God.
I am, I said,
your king.
I am, I said,
your Savior.
I am, I said,
your creator.
I am, I said,
your redeemer.
I am, I said,
your glory.
I am, I said,
the keeper of your next heartbeat.
I am, I said,
the keeper of your next breath.
I am, I said,
not of today,
tomorrow,
or of yesterday,
I am the keeper of all creation.
I stand outside of time,
watching, waiting, for your hearts to come to Me.
For I long to save you.
I long for you to accept My gift of eternal life.
My blood was spilled for your rescue.
The enemy desires to destroy you.
I have come to give you life.
I have come to give you peace.
I have come to give you joy.
I am your king,
the Bright and Morning Star.
The author of your new life,

life from here to eternity.
Remember Me, My child.
I am a consuming fire,
ever-present to be with you.
To love you,
to care for you,
to give you life,
to give you peace,
to give you rest,
to give you life everlasting!

# Redeemed

I am a Christian,
I am a man,
created by God
by His mighty, righteous hands.
I am a Christian,
I am a man,
created by God
for His good pleasure.
I am a Christian,
I am a man,
created by God,
the very expression of His loving-kindness.
I am a Christian,
I am a man,
created by God.
I am His, and He is mine.
I am a Christian,
I am a man,
created by God in His image.
I am a Christian,
I am a man,
created by God
to love, honor and respect him,
to bring forth glory to his holy, precious name.
I am a man,
I fell down,
He raised me up.
I have been bought by a price
with His precious, holy blood.
Yes, we all fall down,
but the Creator Elohim,
Jehovah, my redeemer,
Jesus Christ, the Son of the living God,

He picks me up to sing a new song,
a song of salvation,
a song of love,
a song of peace,
a song of joy,
forevermore throughout all eternity.
Hand in hand with the mighty One
my dearest Lord God and Savior.
I am His, and He is mine,
as I cry out to the mountains high,
the valleys low,
the sky above,
the oceans deep,
I will always forever sing
the song of my precious salvation.
I was bought with a price,
the blood of the Lamb, my Savior, my Jesus Christ.
Restored by His blood,
Word,
and name
forevermore!
Amen!

# Well, I'm Forgiven

Well, I'm forgiven
because of Your loving mercy.
Well, I'm forgiven
because of Your loving grace.
Well, I'm forgiven
because of Your loving hands.
Well, I'm forgiven
because You lived to die,
You died to live
so that I could be with You once again,
hand in hand
in the cool of the day,
in the morning when the dew,
the tears of heaven come down
to kiss the ground,
to give life to the flowers that reach up to the sky,
crying out for all eternity that
You are Lord,
You are God,
You are Savior.
You are the great I Am forevermore.
Yes, I'm forgiven
because of Your loving grace.
Yes, I'm forgiven
because of Your loving hands.
On the cross you stretched out Your hands of love
to the world,
to me,
to the sky,
proclaiming,
"By My very own will,
I surrender My life up for you."
Once and for all, speaking by His crucifiction.

I love you,
I love you,
I love you.
It is finished,
it is finished,
it is finished.
Therefore, by the blood
we have been bought with a great price.
Redeemed,
sanctified,
rescued,
from here to eternity past!

# Where There Is Love

Where there is love,
there is joy.
Where there is joy,
there is peace.
Where there is peace,
there is hope.
Where there is hope,
there is the blood.
Where the blood is,
you have salvation.
Where there is salvation,
you have mercy.
Where you have mercy,
you have grace.
Where you have grace,
you have kindness.
Where you have kindness,
you have Jesus Christ,
the Son of the living God.
When you have Jesus, you have
love,
joy,
peace,
hope,
salvation,
mercy,
grace,
kindness,
gentleness,
patience,
self control.
Where you find all of these, you find Jesus.
For when you find Jesus,

you find the blood.
For by His precious blood
He paid the price
so He could win us back
to have His
righteousness,
peace,
and joy.
He is
our champion,
our creator,
our redeemer,
our God,
our Lord,
our Savior.
He is the mystery unfolded.
He is Christ in us, the hope of glory.

# Yesterday Is Gone

All my yesterdays are gone away
like the fading of the wind.
Yes, yesterday has gone away
like the whispering sands of time.
All my yesterdays have gone away
into the secret place of eternity past.
All my past,
all my sorrows,
all the pains of yesterday
have passed me by since I have been introduced to You
by the Holy Spirit,
my friend,
my teacher,
my counselor,
my joy.
Jesus, my Lord, my God, my Savior, my everything
I thank You for your saving grace, loving mercy.
I thank You for Your precious blood that has set me free
from the chains of death, hell and the grave.
All my yesterdays have passed away into a sea of the past,
a sea of frustrations, never to be seen or heard from again.
All I have now are my tomorrows.
A future of peace, joy, good tidings,
everlasting mercy, grace, an abundance of happiness.

**Scripture:**

Trust in the lord with all your heart,
and lean not on your own understanding;
In all your ways acknowledge Him,
and he shall direct your paths.

Proverbs 3:5-6

# Soldier of the Cross

Soldier of the cross am I. I am, and I will forevermore be, Your faithful, loving, caring, obedient, servant.

No truer words have ever been spoken than these. You will not ever hear of these loyal people on the ten o'clock news. You will not hear of their willingness to proclaim the Holy Word of God. You will not hear of the ones who have lost their lives for the kingdom's sake. The world hates to hear that their evil kingdom is failing. If you look all around you, there is confusion, turmoil, disease, famine, plagues, earthquakes, and floods. If the news would only tell you the truth about how many people were receiving the Lord Jesus as their Savior, you would see what I mean. Don't worry when you hear these terrible things on the news. This only means that we are closer than we have ever been to the coming of our king, our Savior, our loving Jesus who will take us home to be with Him.

**Scripture:**

I charge you therefore before God and the Lord Jesus Christ, who will judge the living and the dead at His appearing and His kingdom: Preach the word! Be ready in season and out of season. Convince, rebuke, exhort, with all longsuffering and teaching. For the time will come when they will not endure sound doctrine, but according to their own desires, because they have itching ears, they will heap up for themselves teachers; and they will turn their ears away from the truth, and be turned aside to fables. But you be watchful in all things, endure afflictions, do the work of an evangelist, fulfill your ministry.

2 Timothy 4:1-5

# Lord, Purify My Soul

Lord, purify my soul
so I can go into this world
with a new outlook on life.
Help me not to see the evil
of all my fellow members of this world,
but to yet respect them one and all
so that I can show forth my goodness
and kindness of heart.
Change me day by day for the better.
Help me to defeat evil so that I can love
only as you would have me to love people.
Help me to think before I speak.
Help me to understand
one and all persons of this world, Lord.
Help me to defeat myself of the evils within.
I surrender to You even my last breath.
Your will be done in my life.
Amen.

# Soldier of the Cross

Soldier of the cross am I.
I am a child of the Most High God.
I am a proclaimer,
a keeper of His holy, precious Word.
Soldier of the cross am I.
I am a child of the Most High God.
I am a messenger,
a keeper of His holy, precious name.
Soldier of the cross am I.
I not only proclaim His word,
I shout out His holy, precious name unto
the highest mountain,
the lowest valley,
wherever He leads me,
wherever He directs,
by the breath of the Holy Spirit.
Soldier of the cross am I.
I am a child of the Most High God.
I have been bought by His sacrifice,
by His very blood.
I have openly decreed to the world
that Jesus Christ is my King,
Lord of all that I am,
keeper of my
heart,
mind,
body,
soul,
and spirit.
I do battle daily, proclaiming His name
and I speak boldly the name of Jesus.
I am not a friend to this world
because I tear down strongholds
so that blind eyes may see

the truth,
the light,
the true kingdom of God.
I am not long for this world.
It does not matter
what you think of me.
It does not matter
if you despise the words I speak with boldness.
It does not matter
if you are offended by the name of Jesus
of whom I proclaim daily
and the King of whom I do serve.
I say to you here and now,
you may be offended by my Lord Jesus Christ,
the Son of the living God,
but remember,
mark my words,
every knee shall bow
and every tongue shall confess
that Jesus Christ is Lord.
Yes, I am a soldier of the cross.
I am a child of the Most High God.
I will,
I will,
I will proclaim openly the Word of God,
the gospel,
the hope,
and salvation of all mankind.
When I die and have left this earth, remember,
I was the one who spoke truth into your life
without hesitation.
Remember,
that I was the one who, by inspiration of the Holy Spirit,
spoke boldly the gospel,
the truth,
the Word of Life,
Jesus Christ.

# Prayer for Salvation

Father God, I humbly come before you in Jesus' name, the Name that is above all other names. Your Word says in Romans 10:9-10 "that if you confess with your mouth the Lord Jesus and believe in your heart that God has raised Him from the dead, you will be saved." Now, Father, I surrender all that I am to You right now in Jesus' name. Thank you, Jesus. I believe I am saved and I will follow You from now and forever. Amen

# SCRIPTURES FOR HELP IN TIMES OF TROUBLE FROM THE WORD OF GOD

# Depression

**Psalm 23:4:**
Yea, though I walk through the valley of the shadow of death,
I will fear no evil;
For You are with me;
Your rod and Your staff, they comfort me.

**Psalm 27:1:**
The Lord is my light and my salvation;
Whom shall I fear?
The Lord is the strength of my life;
Of whom shall I be afraid?

**Psalm 34:4**
I sought the Lord, and He heard me,
And delivered me from all my fears.

**Psalm 50:15**
Call upon Me in the day of trouble ;
I will deliver you and you shall glorify me.

**Isaiah 41:10**
Fear not, for I am with you; Be not dismayed, for I am your God. I will strengthen you, Yes, I will help you, I will uphold you with My righteous right hand.

**Isaiah 50:7**
"For the Lord God will help me;
Therefore I will not be disgraced;
Therefore I have set my face like a flint,
And I know that I will not be ashamed.

**Isaiah 53:5-7**
But He was wounded for our transgressions,

He was bruised for our iniquities;
The chastisement for our peace was upon Him,
And by His stripes we are healed.
All we like sheep have gone astray;
We have turned, every one, to his own way;
And the Lord has laid on Him the iniquity of us all.
He was oppressed and He was afflicted,
Yet He opened not His mouth;
He was led as a lamb to the slaughter,
And as a sheep before its shearers is silent,
So He opened not his mouth.

**Jeremiah 29:11-13**
For I know the thoughts that I think toward you, says the Lord, thoughts of peace and not of evil, to give you a future and a hope. Then you will call upon Me and go and pray to Me, and I will listen to you. And you will seek Me and find Me with all your heart.

**Romans 8:37-39**
Yet in all these things we are more than conquerors through Him who loved us. For I am persuaded that neither death nor life, nor angels nor principalities nor powers, nor things present nor things to come, nor height nor depth, nor any other created thing, shall be able to separate us from the love of God which is in Christ Jesus our Lord.

**Philippians 4:6-7**
Be anxious for nothing, but in everything by prayer and supplication, with thanksgiving, let your requests be made known to God; and the peace of God, which surpasses all understanding, will guard your hearts and minds through Christ Jesus.

**Philippians 4:13**
I can do all things through Christ who strengthens me.

**Philippians 4:19**
And my God shall supply all your need according to His riches in glory by Christ Jesus.

**Hebrews 4:14-16**
Seeing then that we have a great high priest who has passed through the heavens, Jesus the Son of God, let us hold fast our confession. For we do not have a High Priest who cannot sympathize with our weaknesses, but was in all points tempted as we are, yet without sin. Let us therefore come boldly to the throne of grace, that we may obtain mercy and find grace to help in time of need.

**2 Timothy 1:7**
For God has not given us a spirit of fear, but of power and of love and of a sound mind.

**1 Peter 2:24**
who Himself bore our sins in His own body on the tree, that we, having died to sins, might live for righteousness--by whose stripes you were healed.

**Revelation 12:11**
And they overcame him by the blood of the lamb and by the word of their testimony, and they did not love their lives to the death.

Additional chapters in the word of God that will help you to see that you are not the only person who has been depressed:

1. **Elijah:** 1 Kings 17.
2. **Jonah:** Chapters 1-4.
3. **David:** 2 Samuel 11-14.

# Fear

**Genesis 15:1**
After these things the word of the Lord came to Abram in a vision, saying, "Do not be afraid, Abram. I am your shield, your exceedingly great reward."

**Genesis 26:24**
And the Lord appeared to him the same night and said, "I am the God of your father Abraham; do not fear, for I am with you. I will bless you and multiply your descendants for My servant Abraham's sake."

**Genesis 46:3**
So He said, "I am God, the God of your father; do not fear to go down to Egypt, for I will make of you a great nation there."

**Exodus 14:13-14**
And Moses said to the people, "Do not be afraid. Stand still, and see the salvation of the Lord, which He will accomplish for you today. For the Egyptians whom you see today, you shall see again no more forever. The Lord will fight for you, and you shall hold your peace."

**Joshua 1:9**
Have I not commanded you? Be strong and of good courage; do not be afraid, nor be dismayed, for the Lord your God is with you wherever you go."

**Psalm 23:4**
Yea, though I walk through the valley of the shadow of death,
I will fear no evil;
For You are with me;
Your rod and Your staff, they comfort me.

**Psalm 27:1**
The Lord is my light and my salvation;
Whom shall I fear?
The Lord is the strength of my life;
Of whom shall I be afraid?

**Psalm 34:4**
I sought the Lord, and He heard me,
And delivered me from all my fears.

**Psalm 50:15**
"Call upon Me in the day of trouble;
I will deliver you, and you shall glorify Me."

**Isaiah 41:10**
"Fear not, for I am with you.
Be not dismayed, for I am your God.
I will strengthen you,
Yes, I will help you,
I will uphold you with My righteous right hand."

**Luke 8:50**
But when Jesus heard it, He answered him, saying, "Do not be afraid;
only believe, and she will be made well."

**2 Timothy 1:7**
For God has not given us a spirit of fear, but of power and of love and
of a sound mind.

**Hebrews 13:5-6**
Let your conduct be without covetousness; be content with such
things as you have. For he Himself has said, "I will never leave you
nor forsake you." So we may boldly say:

> "The Lord is my helper;
> I will not fear.
> What can a man do to me?"

**1 John 4:18-19**

There is no fear in love; but perfect love casts out fear, because fear involves torment. But he who fears has not been made perfect in love. We love Him because He first loved us.

# Forgiveness

---

**Isaiah 43:18-19**
"Do not remember the former things,
nor consider the things of old.
Behold, I will do a new thing,
Now it shall spring forth;
Shall you not know it?
I will even make a road in the wilderness
And the rivers in the desert."

**Isaiah 43:25**
"I, even I, am he who blots out your transgressions for My own sake;
And I will not remember your sins."

**Psalm 86:5**
For You, Lord, are good, and ready to forgive,
And abundant in mercy to all those who call upon you.

**Matthew 18:21-22**
Then Peter came to him and said, "Lord, how often shall my brother sin against me, and I forgive him? Up to seven times?"
Jesus said to him, "I do not say to you, up to seven times, but up to seventy times seven."

**Luke 23:34a**
Then Jesus said, "Father, forgive them, for they do not know what they do."

**Luke 3:3-4**
And he went into all the region around the Jordan, preaching a baptism of repentance for the remission of sins, as it is written in the book of the words of Isaiah the prophet, saying:

"The voice of one crying in the wilderness;
Prepare the way of the Lord;
Make His paths straight".

## John 20:21-23

So Jesus said to them again, "Peace to you! As the Father has sent Me, I also send you." And when He had said this, He breathed on them, and said to them, "Receive the Holy Spirit. If you forgive the sins of any, they are forgiven them; if you retain the sins of any, they are retained."

## Philippians 3:13-14

Brethren, I do not count myself to have apprehended; but one thing I do, forgetting those things which are behind and reaching forward to those things which are ahead, I press toward the goal for the prize of the upward call of God in Christ Jesus.

## Colossians 3:12-13

Therefore, as the elect of God, holy and beloved, put on tender mercies, kindness, humility, meekness, longsuffering; bearing with one another, and forgiving one another, if anyone has a complaint against another; even as Christ forgave you, so you also must do.

## 1 John 2:1-2

My little children, these things I write to you, so that you may not sin. And if anyone sins, we have an Advocate with the Father, Jesus Christ the righteous. And He Himself is the propitiation for our sins, and not for ours only but also for the whole world.

## 1 John 1:9

If we confess our sins, He is faithful and just to forgive us our sins and to cleanse us from all unrighteousness.

# Grief

**Psalm 23**
The Lord is my shepherd;
I shall not want.
He makes me to lie down in green pastures;
He leads me beside the still waters.
He restores my soul;
He leads me in the paths of righteousness
For His name's sake.
Yea, though I walk through the valley of the shadow of death,
I will fear no evil;
For You are with me;
Your rod and Your staff, they comfort me.
You prepare a table before me in the presence of my enemies;
You anoint my head with oil;
My cup runs over.
Surely goodness and mercy shall follow me
All the days of my life;
And I will dwell in the house of the Lord
Forever.

**Psalm 27:13-14**
I would have lost heart, unless I had believed
That I would see the goodness of the Lord
In the land of the living.
Wait on the Lord;
Be of good courage,
And He shall strengthen your heart;
Wait, I say, on the Lord!

**Psalm 30:10-12**
Hear, O Lord, and have mercy on me;
Lord, be my helper!"
You have turned for me my mourning into dancing;

You have put off my sackcloth and clothed me with gladness,
To the end that my glory may sing praise to You
and not be silent.
O Lord my God, I will give thanks to You forever.

## Matthew 11:28-30
Come to Me, all you who labor and are heavy laden, and I will give you rest. Take My yoke upon you and learn from Me, for I am gentle and lowly in heart, and you will find rest for your souls. For My yoke is easy and My burden is light."

## John 11:25
Jesus said to her, "I am the resurrection and the life. He who believes in Me, though he may die, he shall live."

## John 14:1-3
"Let not your heart be troubled; you believe in God, believe also in Me. In My Father's house are many mansions; if it were not so, I would have told you. I go to prepare a place for you. And if I go and prepare a place for you, I will come again and receive you to Myself; that where I am, there you may be also."

## I Corinthians 1:18
For the message of the cross is foolishness to those who are perishing, but to us who are being saved it is the power of God.

## 1 Corinthians 13:12
For now we see in a mirror, dimly, but then face to face. Now I know in part, but then I shall know just as I also am known.

## I Corinthians 15:3-8
For I delivered to you first of all that which I also received: that Christ died for our sins according to the Scriptures, and that He was buried, and that He rose again the third day according to the Scriptures, and that He was seen by Cephas, then by the twelve. After that He was seen by over five hundred brethren at once, of whom the greater part remain to the present, but some have fallen asleep. After that He was

seen by James, then by all the apostles. Then last of all He was seen by me also, as by one born out of due time.

**Philippians 1:21**
For to me, to live is Christ, and to die is gain.

**1 Peter 1:3-5**
Blessed be the God and Father of our Lord Jesus Christ, who according to His abundant mercy has begotten us again to a living hope through the resurrection of Jesus Christ from the dead, to an inheritance incorruptible and undefiled and that does not fade away, reserved in heaven for you, who are kept by the power of God through faith for salvation ready to be revealed in the last time.

# Epilogue

From the very depths of my heart I have given to you this writing, this piece of my life, the very essence of my being. Do you see the main message that I have been trying to share with you? Jesus Christ, the Son of the living God, is Lord over my life. I would like you to meet Him. Is it not obvious what I am saying through the pen of a ready writer? My statement is this: Day by day, night by night, though your life is like a shadow, you only have one life to live, then the judgement. You must surrender, give up your ways and follow the King of Glory, the very reason we live and we breathe. Give your life to Jesus, for He is the Way, the Truth, and the Life. There is no other way. Jesus came to this earth for a reason. *You were the reason.* He was sent here on a rescue mission to save, to rescue, to free you from this world, the devil, death, hell, and the grave. The Lord has such peace, joy, and abundance for you if you would only trust Him. He shed His holy, precious blood, surrendered His very life, and put your punishment upon Himself so you could be free to live with Him as His little child throughout all eternity. Is that not enough? Give your life to Him. If not to live and breathe for Him, then what else is there? Will you live for money? It will fail you. Are you going to trust in your position of power? In a moment it will fade away like a whisper in the wind. Will you live for another person's love? We all hurt and disappoint each other. No, my friend, if you are searching for a reason to live, the only answer is to live for Jesus Christ, the Son of the living God. He is your answer. Do you want the answers to the devastating problems in your life? Read and study His Word. Therein lies the answers for all eternity. It is His treasure chest of love, joy, peace, and the abundance of life.

This book is for you - the common one, the prostitute, the homeless person, the person hooked on drugs or alcohol, the one in jail or prison who proclaim, "It's all over, time to die." I promise you, it is **not** your end, it is your beginning, if you will only trust Jesus and give your life over to Him.

This book is for you - the one who has known Jesus and walked away because you think He has disappointed you. The enemy has lied to you. He has attacked your mind with false doctrine from others, telling you that Jesus has let you down and that He is not who He claims to be. Jesus has *not* abandoned you. *You* have abandoned *Him*. He is there, ready and willing to take you back into His arms of love, compassion, and forgiveness. The Word of God says in 1 John 1:9 that "If we confess our sins, he is faithful and just to forgive us our sins and to cleanse us from all unrighteousness." I know you have problems. I know there are things in your life you don't understand, but simply come back to Him and trust Him like you did the first time with simple child-like faith.

This book is for you - the one with an incurable disease. Jesus is the healer. Trust Him to heal you. If He decides to take you home to be with Him in all His glory and splendor, then simply rest in what He commands. Even if you should fade away and pass on into eternity with Jesus, is there any sickness or disease in heaven? No, you are healed for all eternity and beyond. Amen!

Finally, this book is for you - the one who has lost a loved one. You cry, you hurt, you have pain, despair and anger. You scream "Why God, why?" "Does God not love me anymore?" Indescribable grief, fear, doubt, and unbelief assault your senses. I assure you, I comfort you with compassion. Jesus is always there with you. He lives within your heart if you are saved, if you are his child. He declares in his Word in John 16:33, " These things I have spoken to you, that in Me you may have peace. In the world you will have tribulation; but be of good cheer, I have overcome the world."

**Scriptures:**

"Come to Me, all you who labor and are heavy laden, and I will give you rest. Take my yoke upon you and learn from Me, for I am gentle and lowly in heart, and you will find rest for your souls. For my yoke is easy and my burden is light."

Matthew 11:28-30

Printed in the United States
By Bookmasters